POEMS and PAINTINGS

A LONG LOVING JOURNEY

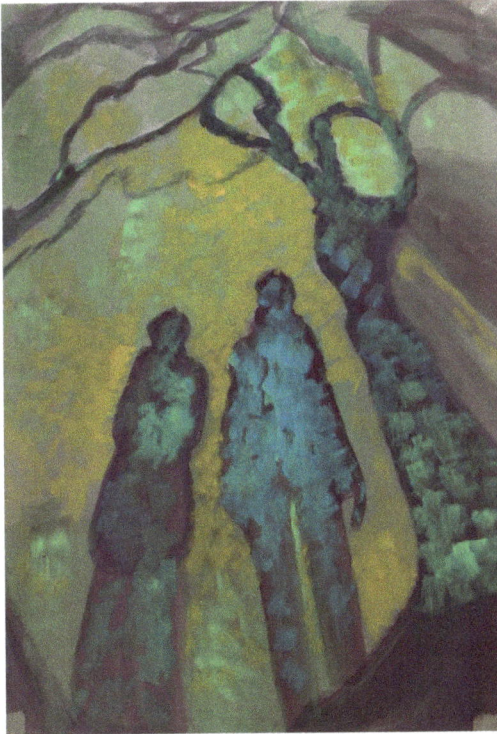

BY EILEEN & MICHAEL SCOTT

Fisher King Publishing

Contents:
Categories, Poems, and First Lines

MEMORY AND MIND

SOUL, SENSE AND SPIRIT

SPECIAL SPECIES

POETRY, ART, AND MUSIC

LAND AND WATER

HOUSE AND HOME

LOVE AND LUST

BEING, DOING, PLAYING

WAR AND WEATHER

STRANGE BEHAVIOUR

MEMORY AND MIND

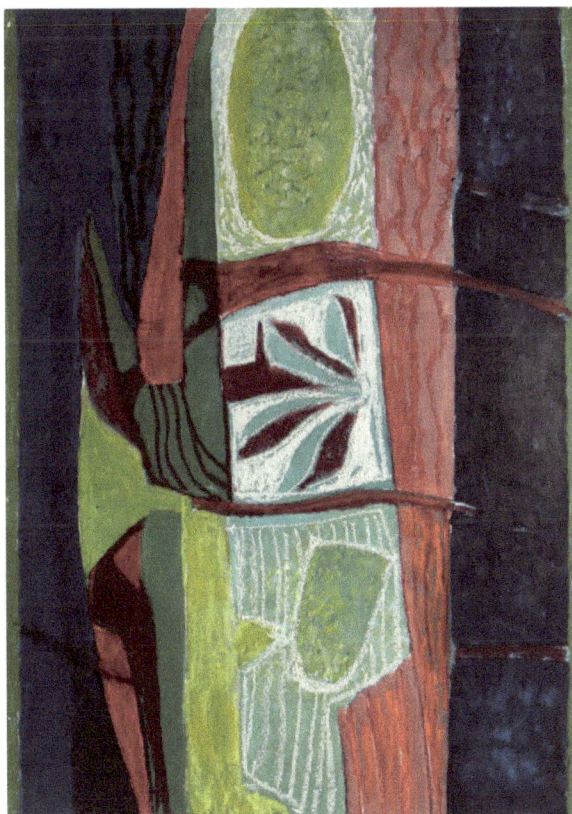

TOUCHING WILD ORCHIDS

Each of us has one shot at the empyrean goal
And we only know that world from being inside;
So I can't tell you, nor you tell me, what it was like
To be in that solitary space, a hole made for one.
Well tell it we may, as if it is describable, as if,
As nothing is, and more than that, we forget it
For ourselves. No description then? No data?
They, who think they know, say: 'childhood is
A unique experience for unique people', and
We think they know something but they don't
Know what I know and I admit it's very little,
A serious shortage of information, hardly worth
A second's thought, you'd think, now you're a child
No more, just a fantasy, a myth, of years so long
Ago that it can't be true, just a foolish whim, just
A story, like that long melted ice-cream, called
By some, the inner child, the poor puer eternus.
Not a chance, not a hope, the child is far beyond.

However, I feel faint sensations, which can't be
Can they, possibly, memories as old as hills
In my aged head, what could linger in this skull?
Why would a nest of neurons remember violets,
White, secret, scented, half hidden in a hedge?
And bluebells on a polished table. And lettuce.
Why lettuce, suddenly? Taste of radish? Toast?
The sensations rush up, the baby sister: death.
Slow worm by her grave, grass snake by pond,
Swimming in pond. Snake in pond. The stream
And bullheads. No thoughts disturb the flow. All
Is sight, taste, smell, song of a bat, the fur of cat,
Pain, blood, arm in sling, tonsils, teeth, the cane.
Still no thinking, did I never think? Not worth a note.
Uncle hitting dad, dad hitting me, mum too. Awake
At night, shaking. Glass marbles. Shooting peas.
Black and yellow caterpillars, striped, red and black
Moths: Deaths-head at window. Gooseberries. Cake.

More and more junk in my small head attic, shrug
My mind with unbelief in me and the space in me
And no end to this forth-pouring of unthink, like ink
Spewing from a cuttlefish, a fish I never saw, heard
Its cry in the sea, where I did not go, no sea for me
Till when to Clevedon, lavender scent, a holiday
Donkeys, Mum laughing, hugging, on sand, pools,
Paddling, a life to live for, like Christmas morning
Once or twice, father laughing, once or twice, must
Have been happy. I did not think. The child in me
Is not for thinking, he consumes the world, takes it
All in, scrumps apples, frees strawberries in woods,
Wild mushrooms in dew, sweet chestnuts secretly.
Soldiers camping in the field, all his nine years have
Waited for this, he loves the regiment, it's home, not
Where his father glooms, where his mum prepares
Food and waits for the baby, he is a wanderer at last;
Nothing holds him now, he can run, he can fly, a bird.

He starts to think. Of all his accidents, the worst, this.
Senses, feelings, reel backwards in the face of words.
Drive comes there: scooter, pedal-car, wooden trolley,
Bicycle: dangerous, accidents, and words spill over all.
Worse to come, words of encouragement, goads made
To make him work-think, to outstand, win, overcome
Sensuality by mentality, to be abstaining, upstanding.
Words engulf the senses, child reels senseless, beaten.
Teenage terror grips, self emerges from the stone, he
Sees now what he is told to see, he learns to know, to
Scrape and bow, he hurts his own feelings, works and
Strains at being good, is angry, apologetic, hesitant in
Love, precipitate in friendship, doubtful in trust, reads
Words as talismans of fortune, believes principles and
Embraces laws. Child hides inside his new ownership,
A king's armour, built to last, visor down, saddled up.
Yet just before adulthood defeated his sweet innocence
He saw and touched wild orchids on the ancestral hill.

WHERE'S THE TIME?

Time and mind climbed Stinchcombe Down
To hear a peal of belling laughter;
Time tripped down and sacked the town
And mind fell grieving after.

Is mind inside its time?
Is time out of its mind?
Both undoubtedly sublime
And both entirely blind

As iodine sublimes into the air
Time dissolves within my ear
The little town, in mind so fair,
My time knows is not there.

Snows of wood anemones would drift
Where bluebells soon would blow:
Flowers and girls were in my gift.
But time and mind had let them go.

As if they never were, time away,
And mind flies up a space, awry:
The never-was holds greatest sway
It is bright delusion to this loving eye.

Grand physics spies uneasily on time at all
Seeing it is not there upon the edge of reason
No wonder my sweet allusions fail and fall
As timely mind goes to the knife of treason.

I think I see that place, the fields, the flowers,
Remembering, if I can, not knowing if I do:
I feed on sandwiches of mind and scented hours,
Ghostly bread on bread and void between the two

Until at last a truth rings out with that invasive bell
The world I think I knew is ephemeral as fears;
It is not time's fault it tripped and broke the spell.
In my mind I made a fancy, a daisy-chain of tears.

BUSY SENSES, IDLE THOUGHTS

Michael Wondered,
As he does:
If no senses would
Mean no consciousness;
Say a person in a coma:
No senses so no sense?
And bigger better senses
Make bigger consciousness?
Do special animals like
Octopi and octopuses
And octopodes, e.g.
Having giant eyes
And hyper brains,
Consequently
Think very big?
Or is there another
Secret function lacking?
And does the brainy squid
Rule its world
Like you and me?
Homo sap. has pride
In its all-embracing
Non-tentacular
Awareness
While people brave
Bad eyes or ears to
Express their inherent
Sentience - think Helen

Keller: arisen.
Take the five
The basics
Their relative importance
As eyes to the artist
And ears to the music-man
Insight to the nun?
Which leads to
Mystic senses
Or telepathy
Extrasensory sensory
And where's the apex
The divine's sense
Of the Divine?
In the brain
Or in the
Supreme
Distance?

NIGHT AND DAY

Are you the One
Or the Two
Does time explain you or merely
Complicate the geometry? Is the linear
What it's all about?
Is time merely a linear measurement?
The clever quantum physicist
Denies time as past or now or morrow
Did I know that Professor Highbrain
Was a guru of the transcendent present?
A mere biologist and even astrophysics-man
Considers time actual and real and here
So all that lives and dies and grows
Whether supernova or pig or periwinkle.
No delusion, then?
Feast-days drift in time, but are defined by time,
As Boeings pass across invisible lines in the ocean
Losing or gaining days at a time.
The beasts know when they're hungry
The bird knows roughly when to sing
The hedgehog knows its winter bedtime
Night and day are real, I'd say
As are spring and winter,
I anticipate the future, for good or ill,
I think I learn from history, mine or yours.
So, really, time is a lie and time is true,
It's in my head and out of it,
In the world and out of it, like fancies,
Time's a crooked mountain track
Along a precipice, a fool's walk in the night
A party piece in the unforgiving day.
I don't have time for this
It's too much for an honest soul
I think I'll take a well-earned rest

NOW AND VOID

Time, a toxin in the stream of my human blood;
Poison from past, future, regret, and yearning
That obliterates the sacred present, the now of being.

It is the Void, the creative emptiness that enables
Time to be transcended, and living nowness found.
So that imprisoned vitality and mystery are unbound.

Time is indeed the enemy, and Void the protector,
Though it is hard for me to understand and fight
The battle my kind and I must face to find the light.

I will not look in the opposite direction for deliverance
Nor perversely seek it in the very coils of serpent-time,
For an unimaginable happiness and a serenity sublime.

I know it is not there, or then, or when, only ever here,
Here in this micro-moment and not expected in the next;
Not anticipated, a blank page in an always empty text.

How often is the moment? Monster-time ensures its rarity:
The Now-and-The-Void are rare visitors to my existence
Kept out of my awareness by my own habitual resistance.

How, then, is it valuable as a pivot of the sacred present
If it is not with me constantly? Surely it should not come and go?
Oh, a permanent and instant present, how I would have it so.

There is a secret here, a deepness not easily seen or realised;
The Void is always with me, it is in my present, always now,
I rest in it, live in its cool embrace, increasingly it shows me how

To withdraw from busy doing, even from busy being, to merge
Into the Void itself, and occasionally still the frenetic pendulum;
The micro-moment slips in ephemerally, and soothes delirium.

It also connects, all with all, the Now-and-Void is the Continuity
Of everything, the inclusiveness of nothing, never specially One:
Diminished time no longer rules, sometimes its day is almost done.

A POEM FOR BOHM

When we were seven years old and relatively real
My memory and I thought we had a lifelong deal:
He thought me, and I remembered him, symbiotically;
So nothing happened in our life together, actually.
But now we've learned about the Implicate Order,
Is everything we remember just a thought-disorder?
First we must explain the other Order, the Explicate,
Say Bohm and Pribram, who often tend to complicate
What we already do not understand, my poor memory
And me, and now we had to comprehend holography.
Can we remember how to do it, make three dimensional
Image with laser, interference, and diffraction, a sensational
Light intensity recording, as if the thing's in front of us
That is a hologram for my memory and me, an omnibus
Of integrated activity translated to memory in our brain.
And so was holonomic brain imagined by the other twain,
Bohm and Pribram, physics and neurology, implicating
And explicating each other, as memory and me, indicating,
A deep and inexplicable gigantic continuity, the holistic all.
My memory thought it through, this writing on the wall,
He was in every cell of my old brain, I could not but agree,
But he, and all memory, was everywhere as well, implicately.
Wrapped up, enfolded, only in consciousness made explicate
So my thinking, my memory said, is only him, whom I replicate.
Tremulously I asked my memory if I had a part in this at all,
Because if my thinking came from him, he was walking tall
While I was an accessory, hanging from his wrist or belt
Did it not matter who I was, what I experienced, what I felt?
I think, with his permission, I heard him laugh, an ugly sound;
But I will still be here, some body, when he cannot be found.

HOLOGRAPHIC MEMORY

A student once was I, with everything to learn.
Anxious to be a knower of the plants, a botanist.
But there was a hurdle, as every flower and fern
Was wearing Greek or Roman words upon its list:
A curriculum of vital information for my degree.
My little grammar school had only mastered Francais,
It was ignominious for me to stand and admire a tree
And hear the competition, loudly and complacently, say
Is it *Quercus robur* do you think, or merely *Q. petraea*?
And how could an enemy of man be *Atropa bella-donna*?
I was stung by *Urtica dioica* and seduced by sweet *Fragaria*
My homage to the great Linnaeus was a badge of honour.
My memory took it in his stride, he simply ate the lot.
But he refused to save me when it came to military law
He said the vacuous Queen's Regulations could go to pot:
I expected to be, but wasn't, cashiered for that small flaw.
He surprised me in business, as he rather lapped it up
Profit, cash-flow, strategy, and leverage, all up his street,
And he really loved the guru food, which he'd gladly sup;
While to make a market presentation he accepted as a treat.
Then when we retired together, he began to go his own way
I introduced him to computers, but he seemed to be insulted,
And when I asked his help with music he declined to play.
He told me he'd had enough of the way he'd been consulted.
I realised he had something else upon his mind, a diversion,
I could not believe a memory would stray into cogitation
I felt usurped by him, it was a most unwelcome conversion.
To make it worse, he seemed to be amused by my agitation.
I searched for words and names, which was properly his task
And he kept getting new ideas, shoving them into my head,
This role reversal was at first disturbing, but now I have to ask
If I would have it any different, when all is better done and said.

MY OLD MEMORY

It's been a long time in the making
This working model of maybe mine
Still learning how to swoop and dive
Perhaps a fish, a frog, a fly, or swallow.
Not me, this metaphorical companion,
More a displaced, wandering phantom
That rests upon me as if I were a tree,
Or leaf of water-lily or wire up in the sky.
How it comes and how it goes, a mystery,
Too misty for my muddled mind, I find
That trusting it as friend is fine, a duty,
More than that, it is inevitability, to be
Memory's dependent slave or even brother,
All the cards are in his hands, no other
Holds me so close, so absolutely, so unfree.
To call my memory mine, a selfish fantasy,
As if I owned a god or devil, sprite or angel,
It is I who is the possessed, held in inner space
By a wayward gravity, a capricious power
That lives and dies in its own time, and I go
Where it goes, and when, and how, so long,
And I go along with it, pretending individuality.
I am, contrarily, an adventitious entity, added on
To my old memory, who is not mine, but me.

THE PATH OF CONFUSION

Human life is a paradox
To be or not to be orthodox:
As the world fights over religions,
Science or religion become bastions,
All forgetting the value of transcendence
With their need for dependence.

Forgetting the universal energy is implicit;
Instead it expresses itself in the explicit
And so goes into deficit
And thus starves our days,
Because of the rule of overarching ways
The journey into being it delays.

SOUL, SENSE AND SPIRIT
Five Poems for the Sensitive Soul

ARISTOTLE'S DRAGON CHILDREN:
THE FAMOUS FIVE

Here there be dragons of multiple meanings.
In this vast sea of consciousness they do breed.
At first there were only five, Aristotle's children:
Dragons of his mighty mind. A mind, supreme
In opinion of itself, with a quintet of scaly senses.
They saw, they heard, they felt, they smelt, they tasted,
And thus he conquered for two thousand years and more.
While consciousness drags its feet, an endless mystery.
But yet, imagine a mind without the senses, as blank
As a lifeless sea, or a laptop lacking a whiff of software.
Could consciousness exist without a jot of input data?
Is there an overwhelming question going begging?
Does mind actually exist except in our imagination?
We either downgrade thinking or upgrade sensing:
We can't have our consciousness cake and eat it.
There's more. It's time to catch the bus of neuroscience.

LOOK AND LISTEN CLOSELY: EYES AND EARS MULTIPLIED

The five old dragons don't give credit for all that we can do:
At least a dozen further senses swim in our internal sea.
There are the Sensors, witty little beasts enabling a sense to be,
They tune in to one specific sensation, a sense within a sense.
In each eye there lie millions of sensors, the rods and the cones.
One hundred and twenty million rods pick up rays of light and
Seven million cones, in three varieties, selectively see colour.
A myriad of senses in each window of the soul, yet there's more,
Before listening to the ear - here, as every student knows, a trinity
Performs: first the gathering of sound to the drum, second to the forge;
The hammer, the anvil and the stirrup gather up vibrations, and third:
To the coiled cochlea and its vibrating hairs, which feed the nerve
That feeds the brain. But, 'miracles never cease', there is another
Sensor yet inside the box, fixed upon the gravitational field, keeping
Constant check on orientation, letting you and me keep balance
In an uncertain world, a sense of stability, where we might fail and fall.

TOUCHY-FEELY ALL OVER:
CONSIDER THE GREAT WHITE SHARK

Predatory we may be, whether for flesh, fowl, fish or truffle,

But think Carcharodon, and fail your primal scream to muffle,

Here's a two-ton killer, called White Death, a true sensory giant.

He can smell a speck of blood in a hundred thousand cc's of sea,

And he can detect a hundredth of half a volt by the magnetic aura

Of his micro-toothy skin. It is enough for him to sense electricity

From a beating heart or a trembling gill in his fearful hidden prey.

Weak are our comparative skills, yet most of these great fish we kill

With our technology and weapons, manufactured senses the gap to fill.

And even we have five or more senses in our skin, severally noting

Heat and cold and pain and itch, pressure, a billion cells for every purpose.

Well they would be called mechanoreceptors, wouldn't they, as if

It makes us any wiser, and spare ourselves the details too? Like the

Ruffini End Organs, Meissner's Corpuscles, Merkel's Disks and to finish,

Charming little thermoreceptors, and dancing follicles at the root of hair?

TONGUE OR NOSE CAN NAME THEE: RECEPTORS AND SENSORS, EVERYONE?

A few more thousand senses to come, and then we haven't finished.
Whose idea was this? 'The five senses', pah! It is a universe at least.
Let us sniff it out, first this nasal cosmos. It is a world of volatility:
Our noses let us recognise ten thousand smelly gases using no less
Than five million olfactory neurons, with supports, stems and cilia
A factory olfactory, the most intimate interface up to the lofty brain.
Now a deep breath, consider: smell is to taste what taste is to smell
Not easy to distinguish effects of nose and throat and tongue because
They have evolved together, a team, with tongue a brilliant invention
Which tastes as a side-line to various other deeply sensual activities.
Taste-buds, then, atop the fungiform papillae, mouthy mushrooms
That swell a little when stimulated, to distinguish the five tastes:
Sweet, sour, bitter, salty, and the Japanese immigrant, umami, which
Is said to be a savoury taste produced by nucleotides and glutamate, q.v.
Ending with a broken myth, the one regarding taste in tonguey sections,
A century-old misreading of the German, you can taste everywhere, try it.

THE BIGGER PICTURE, MOVIE-TIME:
THINGS WE HADN'T SENSORIALLY CONSIDERED

In your muscles and in your joints, sensors jump and buzz
Informing you where your different body-parts reside,
If you didn't know, but how else would you know, except
By looking? Sensors signal motion and tension of muscles;
Information we take for granted yet how else could we do
Important actions, like touching index fingers with eyes shut.
And there's your bladder, sensors there tell it's time to pee,
While big intestine monitoring-units let you know you're full
And, would you imagine, special sensors for hunger and for thirst?
What do you suppose makes your leg go tingly when it falls asleep?
How do you know when you're about to cough, sigh, or sneeze?
More ambitious are they who can sense impending weather-change.
Or feel that they can sense when someone else is looking at them.
Further out, there are wild-card senses of clairvoyance and telepathy.
So when is a sense a part of consciousness itself, not just a messenger,
And how to classify a sense of humour, unfairness, or responsibility?

INEFFABLE REALITY

The tao that can be told is not the eternal Tao
The name that can be named is not the eternal Name.
The unnamable is the eternally real.
Naming is the origin of all particular things.
Free from desire, you realise the mystery.
Caught in desire, you see only the manifestations.
Yet mystery and manifestations arise from the same source.
This source is called darkness.
Darkness within darkness.
The gateway to all understanding.
Lao Tzu's Tao Te Ching (6th century b.c.)

Three friends arguing, as usual, about, of all things,
Consciousness. This invisible grail. Fully void. Sings
Silently. Not for friends. Too intimate for sanctuary.
Fighting friends find a distance. Beyond the boundary.
It starts. He says. 'I am eternal'. Yet is unknown. Erase.
Dismiss the word. 'Eternal' is infinitely not. He says.
No words can be used. His ultimate reality is unknown.
Except he knows it's there. As if it's waiting. Is alone.

In the swim of words a silence surfaces. Language sinks.
He meant, 'all of us'. Three eternal realities, he thinks.
Except he does not know them. Only that they're absolute.
Argument dissolves. A vacant space. The room is resolute.
Its contents, furniture and friends, cat and potted orchidae,
Are one in one sense only: they are not what they seem to be.
Language cannot reveal, except by delicate trick and deception:
A poet's only purpose is to weave the spell of that conception.

FOOD

Food, in three forms, is implicit:
To give life for the body,
To give life for the mind,
And, above all, life for the spirit.
Without food for the body
We starve and die,
Without food for the mind
We cannot fly high,
To make food for the soul
We have contrived a whole
Holy world of religions.
All three foods have led
To gluttony or greatness
Or struggles for power;
So it's still a long journey
That humans must take:
Beyond greatness or greed;
To transcendence in each hour.

GODS AND GARDENS

GARDEN CONVERSATION

She said it was not very different
From when I owned it, when it
Was kept manicured and cossetted
By my devoted and tireless hand
And now, occasionally, lightly tended
And managed by a different mind,
It still held its character if bolder and
A little wild. Mine and not mine. She
Asked if I grieved for it as mine. But
I walked in it every day, I replied. As
If that were an answer. Well it was. To
Just be in it was in a way better than to
Work at it. A change for me. A chance
For me to be really who I am. Maybe.
But suddenly I confessed my true grief.
The life-long love of mine had lost the
Garden and something of herself. She
Would not come to the garden. And she,
I said, was what I really missed, the one
I lived for and still lived with, away from
This garden. Who would not come to it
Now it was not hers nor mine. Simply said
It shook me to my roots, and the woman
Walking with me put her hand gently on
My shoulder. And made my grief blossom.
The garden was beautiful and indifferent.

THE CORNER OF THE GARDEN

The corner of the garden is
A jewel box of brightness and light
Through the conservatory window seen
The wall-peonies: maroon globes
Of brightness and light.
Above the peonies is the pearl bush
Called the bride, with
A mass of white flowers, through
The conservatory window.
The Amanogawa frames the statue
With pink and white branches
It is only April/May
And as it gets warmer
The flowers shed and fade
Relics of yesterday's glory
Jewels that cannot persist
The plants are on their way
To complete their cycle
To produce seeds and fruit
And it is only greed to wish
They would burgeon throughout
The summer and not lose their glory;
Greedily wishing to defy natural reason
By saying this is beautiful
Remain as you are for the
Rest of the season.

GIVING AWAY

I gave way, and gave away my garden yesterday;
It had been years coming, the giving, and the going
Was as easy as it was beyond the limit of my grief
A new emptiness gaped within, a vast wastedness.
For a while, a year or two, it was nobody's patch
Still somehow mine but still somehow not, a watch
For me, a place to stray in, but not mine to stay in
I pulled up an occasional weed, almost furtively,
Half-heartedly suggested small adjustments, fed
The sulking tench, watched the frogs and tadpoles,
Waited for the surging spring of flowers, then saw
At last that I must obey an inner and inexorable law.

It is only five hundred square yards, a handkerchief,
Though crammed with botanical splendours past belief
That's reality, that reality, but not the real reality, one
Buried too deep to comprehend, a land of rain and sun,
Iconic hiding-place, heart-eased by violets and fritillaries,
Coned conifers endure, busy birds, butterflies, and bees
Make it seem a paradise, where transience is memory
And memory a dream, as if everything stays in mind.
But mind itself is temporary, like a garden, pretending
To be eternal, saving the face and grace of mortality
But mind needs a thinker and a garden wants a gardener
And this Narcissus stares into an empty pool, unreflected.

So I gave away a part of mind, I surrendered a memory
I gave myself away, a part I cannot keep, a piece of mind,
A lost half-century, and a relinquished responsibility, gave
Away a paradise I still love and need, but can no longer save.
Is this truly sad, is grief justified, or is it just sweet romance?
The self by definition is self-indulgent, what else can it be?
That garden was not mine, it never was possessed, although
being human, self-important, greedy, I tried to make it so.
As with memory, mind and life, there is a time for all to go,
Could it be possible to lose everything without soul- sorrow?
I look again at the given garden and I realise I really know
It is ruinous to rue, nothing to harvest, even needless to sow.

GARDENING AND GROWING

Gardens are food for the soul:
Sanctuaries of peace and bliss.
Then there's the gardening art
And the beauty depends on this.
The delighted eye of the beholder,
The dreaming, the ecstatic being:
Are enabled by that gracious labour
And that different facility of seeing.
Yet both ways lead to another place
Deeper in the inner mind, or fly
Away outwards, beyond the world,
Indifferent to the question why.
You plan, design, your place of gladness
Where you can dwell in future or today.

Let go your self-importance, celebrate
Your living garden in joyful work and play.
A garden has life in itself and is loved
For itself, but the love can't be forever;
A time will come when we must move on
And the golden connection we'll sever.
There's pain in anticipation too: an old man
Planting roses cannot know if he will live
To see them bloom. And pity he who begins
A young arboretum, that in due time will give
Pleasure, but not to him, he will die too soon.
There is great sadness in longing for his every tree
As it slowly moves beyond his vision, growing
In the living pattern of its own unique maturity.

Can he not care, can he leave it clear, a gift
To the future: a gentle, thoughtful bequest?
Sweet paradox: in separating from the garden
His inner mind could yet be nurtured best.

AND SO TO HERMES

I knew a man, a man who promised miracles,
Who shone with preternatural understanding.
Whose knowledge and intelligence encircled
His small world and ours, his will demanding
That we follow him into self-comprehension;
And the wisp of his will full flowed through
Even in his array of longings, in his condescension
To the followers, we who knew, we who grew
Stronger in his light, transforming our existence,
Lightly godlike, he made an auric field shimmer
Overcoming the sceptic's due and diligent resistance
Without him, life and death have become dimmer.

He was a Hermes, there can be little doubt, although
The similarity was too precise, considering his demerits:
He was a seducer, of minds and bodies, a trickster so
Skilful we hardly know, now, what each of us inherits.
Like the god, he caused catastrophe; to encounter him
Was to court an agony of transformation, this anti-hero
As a psychopomp, led step by step to a psychic interim,
A death, a resurrection, conducted in the depth below.
But he himself was innocent, a child, indifferent to sin,
He journeyed endlessly, inviting those, who dared, to go
Beside him into an underworld of shamanic dreaming
Creating his new world, in which the word could grow.

Now his light has died, his creations and his victims lie
On uneasy beds, now unsure of how and where to travel.
As does the mythic god, the mythic man still tells us why
There are no mysteries nor beguiling enigmas to unravel
There is only a momentary being to consider, to see and feel,
To breathe eternity in a fleeting gasp, and no wheel to deal.

MYTHS ARE MYTHS. NO? YES?

A myth, by semantic definition, is without foundation
So how can you tell a good myth from a bad one?
Greeks for instance have now a devalued economy
But is it fair to see their old top god Zeus as enemy
Of reason, yet swallow Jesus, Allah, and Jehova?
An impossible hedge for an open mind to get over.
What makes the latest fashion in divinities move on?
What happens when the thrill upon the cat-walk is gone?
Who decides the new blue is green, or white is black?
High heels or flatties, short skirts or leggies, hot pants,
What hidden siren voice makes mad cleric prince of rants?
Then there's Waldemar on TV, mixing images like mad
Jesus looked like a pretty Athens lad with curls, how sad,
Till he turned into a snarly Zeus complete with darkling beard
Mythic only means they've made it up, precisely as I had feared.
But then, is not all so-called knowledge myth. How is it known?
Surely just a tale of old wives, a barefaced lie that's sown
And grown in the fertile compost of hope and need, leave
It lying, lying still, until, it grows and grows till you believe
Sometime, somewhere, it was true if only you knew how.
So, Olympus and Holy Land are one, even though they row,
Zeus and Hermes, mighty once, have dwindled to mere fame
While Jesus and Mohammed have played the winning game.
In truth, the myths of Athens and Jerusalem are all the same.
The Vatican and Mecca, Lambeth Palace, and the synagogue,
Are they supermarkets of food, goodies the masses love to hog?
Does it matter? Is there a truth to hanker after, something real?
Or is this microscopic planet truly, truly, crazy; and no big deal?

THE EDEN PROJECT

And Adonai said, 'What is the date today?' Heaven shook with fear;
An angel whispered in the Holy Ear, 'There is uncertainty, dear Lord
God of All. I think your Bible says it's Monday, April first, eight thousand.'
'Eight thousand what?' Jaweh roared. The witless seraph cried, 'I think BC.'
'We don't know about Jesus yet,' Jehova said, 'And, I put Aborigines on earth
Eighty thousand years ago, so are you talking decades instead of years?'
The angel, an ancestor of Dorothy Francis Gurney, was lost for numbers.
'And, another thing,' Odin shouted, 'That blasted Bible isn't written yet, it
Has to wait for me to make Adam and break his rib. No, that can't be right!
Not with black men already in Australia and into Africa.' Then He slumbers.
He dreams. He thinks about his heart. And his divine nature. And Eden.
Allah is bored. And not getting any younger. It's time for the grand jesture,
Or jester, he's not sure which, with time and space a macrocosmic mess.
Lilith slid alongside the sleeping deity, kissed him with her snake's teeth,
And he knew passion as never in his life before. But Elohim was not a man:
Envy sprang into his mighty breast, he vowed to make mad Adam suffer;
And everything else, come to think of it: he'd fill the earth with misery.
'I declare its eighty thousand years BC', he proclaimed, 'Before my son,
My fatherless son, purely wrought, shall suffer execution in my name.'
But he was still bored. What would he do for eight hundred centuries?
'I know,' said he, 'I will amuse myself with cosmic gardening, I will
Make that little globe a hell of invention, millions of living monsters,
Eating each other, I will send typhoons and earthquakes and floods,
A grand endeavour, the trees will be firewood, the seas will boil, such
Will be my garden of delight, it will lighten up the firmament, irradiate
My universe, and in the middle will be man and woman, replete with sin.
And they will praise me, call me Loving Father, thank me for my grace.
In my garden, they will hear the holy heartbeat, but never see my face.

MY FATHER'S GARDENS

My father's house has a garden that is like his house.
The vegetables are tidy, lawn and hedges well-shaved.
There is a shed in it, with coal, and tools and my bicycle
Which is welcome there, despite its being mine, his gift.
I love his lettuces and carrots and great cold cabbages
I love his shed and its infinite variety of order;
And around the squares of grass are pale yellow tulips,
Sweet-smelling carnations, stocks and lilies-of-the-valley.

Around the new house of my father we make a garden such as
Rich men have: sky-scraping trees, a lake, an orangery, terraces,
Languid nymphs, Olympic heroes, avenues, temples, bridges
Over a trout-full stream, aviaries, orchards, gazebos, conservatories.
Here he walks, smiling, radiant with the mystery of it all
Nothing and everything his, as it always was, a humble man,
Anxious to be entranced. We work together. I show him
My joy in flowers, he holds them to his heart.

THE GREEK GIFT OF JESUS

The story of Jesus is Greek to me,
I mean it was written in Greek.
I cannot read Greek and am grateful
For the maybe accurate translation;
But it is still Greek to me, unless I
Retranslate it, into Greek mythology.
I can understand the antics of Zeus
And his wife, Hermes mother, Maia,
Though the little godling could have
Been a chick, swan-necked, web-footed.
I can follow all the fun about stealing
Apollo's cattle, sibling rivalry, hardly
A myth at all, just a happy, crazy, family.
But the Greek who invented Jesus had
Different fish to fry. He, or she, whoever,
Plagiarised Epicurus for the new morality
(Without acknowledgement, the cheapskate)
And found an oven-ready meal for souls
At lunch on the real or imaginary Olympus.
Go compare Jesus and Hermes (or Apollo):
Too many similarities for even synchronicity.
There's the story, Jesus from Olympus, Gold
Medallist of good deeds, Mills and Boon
Couldn't beat it. A publishing sensation.
But Jesus had a stunning finale, Harry Potter
Plus, while Hermes only made a merger with
The Egyptian wizard known as Thoth. Though
Either way, this pair of mythic guys, Jesus/Hermes
Booked into forever, some strategy! Some trick!

SHAGGY GOD STORY

First I grow myself a garden
Then make two people for it.
There is a snake, also the devil,
Balanced, naturally, by angels.
But trees are my speciality,
My secret nickname is Arborigod.
For the couple I have arranged
A Tree of Temptation, just for me
To see if they will or won't obey
My instructions; I made them free
To eat the fruit of Good and Evil.
My will is absolute, I say, but they
Must be autonomous to do as I say.
There's actually nothing special on it,
Eating from it would have no effect
Upon their knowledge. It is just a way
Of testing their obedience, I need
To know I am supreme, that I rule
In their hearts and minds, a divine will.
But they eat the fruit, and so see sin.

That's it, I say, I am divinely enraged.
I punish everybody, for ever and ever,
I fill the world with everlasting sin. I make
Their children and their children's children
Suffer sickness, madness, death, terror,
And everything horrible till the end of time.
So ask me why I let the Devil tempt them.
I had to, by my will they had to choose,
Not my fault they chose wrong. I'm God.
After all. I must have my way. Otherwise
I might appear too weak. And I'm strong.
My only regret is that my son had to pay
For Adam's arrogance, a sacrifice too far,
But I had to protect my reputation, give
A little, as we say, in heavenly circles.
The masses on earth can be redeemed
By the glorious crucifixion, what an icon!
Yes, indeed, but it makes me wonder if,
Given the sin in human nature, if my lad
Hasn't got too popular, it makes me mad.

KNOWING
A Biblical Exchange

Master, how shall I know what to know?

The other-knowing are wise

Master, how shall I know that I know?

The self-knowing are discerning

Master, how can I become strong?

Those who triumph over others have muscle

Master, how can I become revered?

Those who triumph over themselves are commanding

Master, how can I become wealthy?

Those who know what enough is are affluent

Master, how can I become secure?

Those who practice strenuously have resolve

Master, how can I achieve survival?

Those that don't lose their place are enduring

Master, how can I become eternal?

Those who die and don't disappear are long-lived

Source: *Tao Te Ching*

THE HOLY BIBLES
(A BABBLE OF BIBLES AND A GAGGLE OF GODS)

The human mind, crammed with gods and holy books:
Nothing like it anywhere on earth, what went wrong?
Man is a medium-sized mammal, late in primate line,
With an exceptionally large brain, too big for every day,
A weak creature with supernormal cerebration, asking
For trouble, and getting it, nearly extinct for centuries.
It wasn't shamanic enthusiasms that saved its day
But cleverness like crops and herding, tools and trade.
When did the godness begin? A contagious insanity?
Did it start with accidental connections? Sacrifices
And rising suns? Or was it collective narcissism, pride,
The first dread inklings of celebrity culture, an egotism.
Was the mind a cup that ranneth over, spilling fetishes.
How many hundred gods has that mad mind created?
Uncountable and unaccountable, how many, and why?
Gorillas, orangs, chimps, and monkeys do not do it.
All the hominids and extinct humans may have done it.
People certainly do it, worship, sacrifice, dance, make
Innocent others do it, and making them change gods.
And so it came to pass, that millions of humankind had
Fewer and fewer supergods, by amalgamation or culling.
An indefinite number, as opinion varies about the status
Of this god or that, but it's probably ten times ten today.
And therefore some hundred bibles, plus or minus twenty,
Depending on what qualifies as big and holy, writ large,
And some bibles have fifty books or more, out they pour.

One bible outsells all the rest, year after year, billions;
Maybe zillions, but there are a lot of Christians to buy
What is described by Christian authority as, 'a collection
Of sixty-six books, by forty authors, in three languages,
On three continents, over roughly sixteen hundred years.'
A deluge of bibles, then, and a conglomeration of cults.
Take two billion Christians, in how many Christianities?
The answer, my friend, is forty thousand variations on
A theme of sin, sacrifice, redemption, and resurrection.
Why, oh why, oh why, has the big-brained biped opted
For a myriad ways of supernatural excess, mostly,
And why are millions unconvinced, maybe ten per cent?
Laterally think the question, it's got to be the brain, not
To say we're crazy even if we likely are, well must be.
Consider the human nervous system, all those neurons
About a hundred billion each, focusing on fight or flight,
Awareness of prey, predator, foe, friend, mate or rapist.
We are a species shot through with fear and fear and fear,
We need a big protector, or protection from the unknown
Predator that may lurk here and there and everywhere, we
Are sore afraid. And afraid to be afraid, fear grows on fear,
An individual mountain of unbearable anxiety. Something's
Got to give in the neural net. We can't take existence as is.
It must be something else, a better place must exist for us
Considering how wonderful we are, the pain must go away
Please take our pain, someone, something, and recognise
Our worth, especially to you, we'll do anything to adore you
If you'll take care of us, your special children, big father.
It is a massive contract, done with the lord of the universe
In our neural net, the seat of knowledge and awareness.
It can't just be a big mistake, can it? Are we not worth it?
Are we not a special creation? The bibles say it's so. Believe!

MORALITY AND MORTALITY

SELECTIVITY

I have, you will discover, selected you to be
The recipient of affection of such a one as me.
Undoubtedly, I think, you soon will clearly see
The creation of an entity we will describe as 'we'.
Why?
Funny you should ask. I felt sure you might.
As I've reason to believe that you are fairly bright.
The answer is, research, consider it in that light;
I've studied you intensely so I know that I am right.
Really!
Sounds rather formal? And one-sided? Oh I do agree.
But in my heart I am behaving most empathetically;
I speak so coolly just to ensure that you feel free
So let me put it to you, as if it were a modest plea.
Reasons?
Yes, you would ask that, being first person cerebral.
Oh dear, analysis always makes me feel so terrible.
All right, here goes, your virtues first, so shareable,
Then your little vices, all completely sweet and bearable.
Mine?
It's not for me to say, as I am selecting you, not me,
However, if you want to communicate assertively
I will obtain for you an independently compiled CV.
Meanwhile, allow me to continue my friendly homily.
If you must.
Such accomplishments, they might even be too great
For any ordinary friend to manage on their meagre plate;
Even I admit to some concern that I could bear the weight
Of daily confrontation with your superiority of state.
Too good-looking

Some might say
Too brilliant
For ordinary minds
Too articulate
For tied tongues
Too erudite
For ignorant folk
Too lofty
For lowly souls
Too rich
For frugal drudges
Too confident
For downcast hearts
And much
Too much for eyes of green.
How fortunate you are to find me,
I am that rare person without envy;
How glad am I to meet my dear ally
One with whom I can fly on high.
Vices?
I had forgotten, dwelling on your brilliance
But, yes, the balanced view, dear friend: askance;
I look upon myself to even think you by chance
Lacking any quality of mind or spirit. You enhance:
Too clear, my vision of you,
Beyond the sight of fools
Too compassionate, for your,
Suffering, which only I can see,
Too tolerant of your pride
That ordinary minds misconstrue
Too profound my understanding
Of your bitterness,

Too transcendental my higher mind
Regarding your straying self
Too loyal in my faith
To belittle you as others do
Too generous in my being to
Let peccadilloes overturn the scales
You are, you see, quite safe with me.
What rot!
Oh, no, now that is too vicious
Even for my magnanimity
I will leave you to contemplate
The opportunity you so flippantly
Disregard without even waiting
To see my independently compiled
Extremely impressive, outstanding,
Even glorious CV
Yes, perhaps you have a point
Maybe I've had a fortunate escape,
But such is friendship it never quite
Lives up to its exquisite hope and promise
Good wishes, then, in gentle disappointment
I wish you well in your search for joy
Oh, such pity do I feel for us, indeed for we;
You seemed so perfect to me, for me.

THE FIRST WOMAN

She is a perfect picture of charm and cosmic dismay
And maybe that is as it always was for her, underneath
Serenity, steadiness, the sureness of touch and mood.
There is a catastrophe in there somewhere, hiding its face.
An arid family way back, the un-joyful years of work, not
So unusual, we all make do with what we choose. And then:
She burst into flower, lived a new delight, found her way.
At her zenith, in her beauty, in her power, there it was:
She discovered the inner grail, the secret, ubiquitous energy
Joining her to the other, whoever, with transformational force,
And her true tribe, true leader, true vocation, true bliss.
How could this have faltered? What dark angel drew a sword
That cut the umbilicus, killed the child before it could fully grow?
Deaths did not help, her leader lost, nor the jealous scepticism
Of her struggling mate; yet it seemed an inner doubt, as if
It was really all too good to be what she needed it to be, a truth.
That is, a truth too great to be sure of, an untrustworthy yearning
For an everything she could not quite believe. And so she fell.
And fell again. Tripping, slipping, shaking, breaking her body,
Breaking maybe her heart. Or because her heart was breaking.
Her paintings are there for all to see, her books for all to read,
Did her munificence drain that flow of shining energy, or did she
Sink into the quicksand's of doubt, as now it seems, her fateful
Animus hating her un-wellness, her weakness, her dependence,
Her loss of interests, her boredom, wistfulness, and what thing
It was that laid her out, and this incessant flatness of feeling.
The time is now, now the time, for her to make a new embrace:
All is still in her, spirit, compassion, empathy, refusal to be

Bamboozled, dislike of tawdriness, of sleaze, and of unkindness.
She almost sees her shame and guilt are unwarranted, and that she
Wastes time just holding on, and she must know she is now ready
For the leap into comprehension, where her trust still waits for her.

THE TRIALS OF JULES MCAVARICE

They blamed his impoverished youth
For his greed and excessive ambition
Yet it seemed merely constitutional
And just a natural predisposition.

First he acquired a high education,
Freely given by the state at that time,
Then he wed a well-bred young woman
With whom he'd have happiness sublime.

Next he sought after fortune and fame
The expected objects of alpha-male lust
And decided to become a business tycoon
For rewards pure and legal, so fair and so just.

Then came all those manly jewels, sweet icing
On the newly baked cake of his masterful self;
The watch by Omega, opulent cuff-links, a tie-pin
Of diamond and gold, backed by a surfeit of pelf.

With the obligatory wardrobe designed for his wife
And the sycophantic soft purr of his Bentley in blue
Plus the sweet little flat for the new love of his life
Jules McAvarice was the richest of a very small few.

As his drinking companions observed and discussed,
Jules, if not exactly unhappy, obviously pined for more.
What more could he possibly need, on top of the upper crust?
Was there a parvenuous rot in his secretive tycoonic core?

He fancied perfect immortality, naturally, a basic human right,
And reincaration too could be an interesting holiday now and then,
But how could he escape the suffering that came visiting every night;
That ghastly demon succubus seducing him: again, again, and again.

She described him as irresistible, making him unsure that he was,
She named him the idol of all women, and the envy of all persons.
While not really surprised he'd hoped to keep that a secret, because
Their desire and their jealousy might endanger his cosmic ambitions.

Was it to be God, or merely Great King of the World. Or preferably both?
If neither yet existed, he could create both positions, a fine Double First.
Then his head filled the bedroom. He awoke with a blasphemous oath.
Awake and unsure of his supremacy. Jules the Blessed and Jules the Accurst?

He became haggard, looking haunted and old, far beyond his years
As the evil female in his dreams dragged him further and further down.
His wife and his children left him, his businesses bust, he was full of tears;
Friends full of schadenfreude said he was harvesting what he'd sown.

The wages of sin, they cried, saying 'Covetousness brings its own reward'
The greed of man shall visit plagues and terrors upon his house, thy god
Will not be mocked, return thee to poverty, surrender all, take up thy sword,
Fall thee upon it, free thy laboured soul, let thy corpse rest beneath the sod.'

Jules considered options, reviewed his life, realised his greed had vanished
And thought how much he missed his children and longed to see his wife.
He gave away the car and jewels, sold the redundant mansion. He banished
His ambition, and now his envious heart turned towards the saintly life.

Francis of Assisi seemed a likely paradigm, another rich man turned poor,
Repudiating worldly life, the first stigmatic, famously animal-loving, saint,
Everybody's friend, street-preacher, and opener of the environmentalist door;
Jules could copy Francis and be famous for being a simple man without taint.

Better still, up the intellectual chain, uncompetitively of course, emulatively,
Jules aka Jewel would shine brightly as a thinking man's guru, the new Bede.
Or even Anselm or Eckhart. A modern Humanist, a friend of god relatively,
Bringing the weight of thoughtfulness to the ancient dictatorial creed and deed.

Thus The Jewel of Avarice, of man and god compounded, a man beyond price;
The light of reason shone about him, he bore the marks of humility and pain.
In this dark world, where rapacity and exploitation rule, with scant opposition,
The likes of Jules McAvarice will appear, without doubt, over and over again.

'Ad infinitum ad nauseam', I fear.

THE AGES OF MAN

A cliché for our age, as in the time of medieval minds,
A fixation on age itself, and preference for youth; now
The industry of anti-time lifts faces, tucks flesh, denies
The process that might make us whole, namely, growing up.
Another time, another place, oriental minds worshipped
Wisdom, which took time to grow, a journey into being.
Not so for errant knights encased in plumed and shining
Iron, as modern warriors, ego-armed, subdue the world.

Poor Parzival shows the way: clever-killing champion
And foolish child, learned late to find his internal grace
And recognise the emptiness of outer pomp and power
His downfall was his epiphany, his new reality was born.
A long, long search, around ages and beyond, begins
When the seven ages reduce to one, in the present being.
All the outer world can no longer stage the play: when life
Becomes a personal inner space, a universe of radiance.

BLING-BLING, SIN-SIN.

1.

Equivocation is the golden rule for judgement by the people
The prince and his mistress are sweet objects of rabid admiration
And just as much derided for their minor faults or major sins.
Ah, saccharine equivocation, memory of a sun-kissed king, our
Own Edward, Albert, Christian, George, Andrew, Patrick, David,
Sacked ignominiously for his love of older, married, women, one
Especially, and if he lost his youthful gloss, his brother had none,
Nor the niece who has somehow held her subjects' close attention,
Lover of dogs and horses and mother of an unstable brood while
Sturdily transporting her jewels, occupying her palaces, and riding
Up to Parliament dressed like an ancient Christmas Tree to hector
The Republic with Royal words coined by civil citizens of grace.

2.

Plus ca change, moins ca change: this Saxe Coburg Gotha aka Windsor,
Might as well be old King Croesus for all the difference between them.
Power and riches go hand in glove, especially with clever advertising,
And only greater power can prevail, theoretically even the poloi, you,
And I, but actually not. Hitler nearly did, with a million storming troops,
An American General and President ditched the British empire. Big guns
For big targets. And so it was with a great Roman, Crassus the Crass, a
Super-ass, vain and arrogant like our own Edward, but richer and cleverer
And a self-made man to boot, a hard man, fed on greed, a special breed
In BCE sixty-three. But the methods are the same. Give or take a lottery
Or a talent-show or two, or a flutter with someone else's savings; whereas,
Crassus traded real estate, slaves, and silver, with full and frank extortion.

3

Plus ça change indeed. A lot of luck as well: the famously infamous Sulla
Killed ten thousand men and took their property. Then he gave some to
Guess who? Marcus Licinius Crassus, that Who, and the Dives made a mint
By his private fire service and fingering owners as their properties burned.
Crassus made one big mistake, in his super-ass period, aged sixty-one.
Amongst his many talents he was a fair military man, for one example
He was the man who put down slave Spartacus in the third 'servile' war.
Not an easy victory and some might say it was better lost, less ignoble.
Then Dives teamed up with Pompey and Caesar, such a clever move,
To make the First Triumvirate. Crassus was the banker. Caesar skint.
Crassus was rich and powerful, yes, but was greedy for greater fame.

4.

That one mistake, then: there's always one to make the gods seem real,
They that would destroy a man and firstly drive him mad, apparently.
The signs were portentous; a feast upon ten thousand tables and giving
Enough grain to feed all Rome for ninety days, Crassus showed his world,
Showed he was the richest and the maddest of all men, and now sought
The ultimate victory in battle by invading Parthia in fifty-three BCE.
He lost the day, and thirty thousand men, against superior intelligence -
And the terrible armoured Parthian archery in the desert plain of Carrhae.
So Crassus died, made to drink molten gold, a Parthian joke, then beheaded.
The real mistake, his failure to see the emptiness of his own ambition, was
The blueprint of rulers who place petty power and prestige above all else.
Look around, at the vanity of fools on thrones, and pity the Crassus clone.

A BIBLICAL ANECDOTE

And God said, 'Let there be Greed'.
And Adam on Apple began to feed.
Dutifully fulfilling his master's creed.

God also induced the first lady to sin.
So lust and gluttony could also begin.
And God provided avarice, with a grin.

Eden entertained the Holy Peeping Tom.
He subdivided avarice into a list so long;
Even a saint could easily go very wrong.

Disloyalty, betrayal, bribery and treason,
For example, God offered for no good reason.
Just an amusing sacrifice for every season.

Not to be outdone, God had sins of his own.
Really big ones, well-fed and overgrown.
His need for love was cosmically overblown.

He commanded men and women to multiply
So that divers offspring could grow and fortify.
And they who failed to praise him he would mortify.

His pride required obedience, martyrdom, and devotion.
However mortals suffered he demanded positive emotion.
For a millennium or so, he niched this crazy notion.

At last, inevitably, other Gods came trading on his territory.
He had to rebrand Himself to hold his dwindling viability
Even so, for some, His reputation became a marketing liability.

LITTLE GREEN GIANT

Love is nice, truth is good, and beauty cuts the mustard,
But the big money gets put on that druggy green custard:
It tastes of heaven, makes you mad, comes sweet and bad
To your eager mind, blind with greed, squirming, glad.
It's lovely, slurpy, this: a vicious, viscous, invidiousness;
Though Bertrand Russell said it caused exceptional unhappiness.
How would he know? Maybe he went in for it big-time
He was a lefty, after all, for whom everything's a crime.
You know it comes from lack of self-esteem, envy does,
A 'narcissistic personality disorder', the current buzz.
Then there's the other side of it, sneery schadenfreude,
Getting kicks from others' pain, misfortune and murder.

Like sadomasochism, envy, is a madness, to put it mildly
What to do about you, my friend, when you're behaving wildly?
My heart is yours, and yours is mine, a comradeship to die for -
We share vital blood-pumps, it's you and me we should adore.
There is that greenish glint, and weasel words to oil the wheels,
Sincerest form of flattery'! kiss my nether regions! It just feels
A crappy competition, sickening miasma from a putrid ego.
Never envy that dear friend, oh no, just kick the stupid so-and-so.
If it comes to showing-off, clever-clogs can be outshone, undone;
Sharp-barbed arrow from the put-down quiver whizzes into one
Or other of us, blood gushes, love spills out, friends again at last?
Life's too short for truth, beauty dies young, envy may have passed.

HANG ON TO YOUR JEWELS, MAN.

Hang on and think on, O Mister,
I speak to you as a blighted sister:
And when I look at you it's a fool I am seeing
Strutting his mad stuff as a superior being.
Whether stupid or clever, strong or cissy weak,
Makes no odds, your mentality is a fecking freak.
Why, you would ask, if you had moral sense,
Are women and girls so abysmally dense
That they can't do something to improve their plight,
Something to sharpen their limited sight?
The reason, damned brother, is the way you fixed it,
Your bloody gender set it up as a cosmos of bullshit.
It's all in your tribal insanity, that honourable name,
It's your name and you will kill for it, and breed with it.
And cover the earth with it, always the same mad game.
You don't care, so long as your tribe's jewels hang over it.
Ah, those family jewels, the sparkling hegemony, the same
Treasured organs rule in spires and minarets, in markets
And monasteries, counting houses, war rooms and prisons.
Yes, brother, sometimes a woman forgets her place, gets
A tyrant's hat, a monarch's mantle, the jewels in her grip
But she's only borrowing, a man can cut her down and does.
O woman, you are the man that never was, nor likely to be,
You are too divided, and not convincing as a man, the HE
WHO SQUAWKS LIKE A COCK:
'I AM GOD, BOW DOWN TO ME'

I MET A MAN ONE DAY

I was walking, innocently, in a secret leafy wood,
When I heard a sharp soliloquy, a voice quiet yet acidic
And came upon a hermit in his lair, a misanthrope,
He appeared, yet apparently happy in his isolation,
And he smiled and glared at me, continuing his rant,
He beckoned me to sit with him, and addressed himself
To me, as if he recognised a friend. This is what he said:

I don't like it here, you know, I did not exactly choose it,
But there was all this madness about sin, sin and more sin;
I had to get away from it. I am suffering, for sure, misery
Is mine, but just like all the other beasties in this wilderness
I am free from sin. You understand the difference? It's bad
To be a beastie, all of us I mean, all creatures great and small
Don't really have a chance at all in nature red and raw.

Who invented sin, I want to know, what idiot theotwat?
It must be the moron who dreamt up hell and such Godwhat.
But how did a mental ailment become a worldwide mania?
Not Buddhists, not even ancient Greeks, mad as they might be,
Made life more foul by adding blame to agony. 'Tis insane.
All the other animals would laugh at us, if they realised that
We daft humans demonised the simple pleasures of a dog or cat.

Think, friend: lust, gluttony, and greed, three happy little things
Keep the juices flowing and save the animals from extinction.
Laziness never hurt any creature, and envy is only competition.
I don't think much of pride, myself, but lions seem to like it.
And now you'll say I have the sin of anger, I suppose, going on
Like this; well I'd readily own up to that, but I say it ain't no sin,
To rail against hypocrisy, self-righteousness, the whole pious din.

I left him in his woody den, and pondered his point of view
And found I could not fault it. Dogless as I am, I considered
Instead the nature of my cat, and could not find him faulty.
A sinful cat is truly a ridiculous notion. And the sins of humankind
Cannot bear examination. But then I wondered. Anger is unpleasant
And angry cats and dogs may leave their mark upon the flesh.
But lies and castigation make scars upon the vulnerable mind.

There's the sin, then, the poison to the spirit, the cant of priests,
The threat of unending damnation, the fire and brimstone of
Lutherans and Catholics, the vengeance of a jealous God, the
Murder of his son, these are sins visited upon men by ministers,
Celebrated in burnings and tortures, they are the sins of God
Made manifest in evil men. And my cat sits on the mat and smiles
A holy smile, a better creature than most of us by a million miles.

PLEASE KILL ME

Gently, with love, no pain, no sermons, just a favour
Is all I ask, I want a moment of great joy, a taste to savour;
Save me as I saved my cat of grace, with grace, as he purred
Against my chest, held, soothed, as his pain was softly cured.
Pain is cheap and handy, I can do it for myself, DIY Defeat:
Garotted, drowned, brain bulleted, twenty floors to concrete,
Poisoned, gassed, throat-slashed, bussed or trained, brained
Or flamed in petrol, it's all legal, self-administered, stained
With sin for some, just blood and bits of me I anticipate, grim
Exit from grim world, worst deal possible, insane, immoral, dim,
Is my irrelevant opinion, the powers be beyond me, fellow fools
Who set the rules, the English Inquisition, those po-faced tools
With thumbscrews in their souls, 'Thou shalt be tortured as God
Decrees, and so shall any man that helps thee, thou sorry sod.'

Assisted Suicide, the crime of choice for me, 'Please Kill Me'
Isn't much to ask, you'd think, said and done pleasantly.
Of course it might be murder by mistake, as the surgeons do,
But anaesthetics and good intentions make that all right too.
Nothing's perfect unless everything is perfect which it really is
So death is nothing much is it? There's a lot of it about, in this
Place of natural mess and bother, and there's them who'd tidy it
If they could, and who keep on trying, who want to do their bit
For law and order and make their views into rules, like I can't die
When and how I want to die, theoretically, and so I have to lie
And cheat my way to sweet oblivion, or travel to a killing clinic
And die the stupid death of an ignominious and foolish cynic;
What about my bloody so-called human rights, is that a scam
Like everything else on this poor earth, and do I give a damn?

FABLES AND THEIR CHIMAERAS

The truth they say will set you free,
But lies and fables are so comfy:
Seeing the world just as you please
Walking the ways without a shadow, where
Nymphs and unicorns and heroes come.
But should there show up a fiery dragon
You may wield the lance of the noble saint.
However, fables have their seamy side
Especially when gods become involved
Then heroism often is a sorry plight
Such as when a grumpy heavenly dad
Kills his fabulous only son upon a cross
Or that maladroit idiot deity, Zeus, chains
The Titan to a rock to make a daily meal
For his semblance as a charismatic eagle.
Watch out, too, for sundry other chimaeras
Like bull-headed madmen in their labyrinths.
By the time you've had your fill of fame
And glory, pain and self-regard, think, now
Is the truth really such an inferior deal?

MRS BURROUGHS AND XMAS

Cars and busy buses hum,
And pedestrians try not to run.
Berried holly is a hymn to the sun;
Tomorrow, families join to make fun.

Mrs Burroughs steps from the pavement,
Two loaves or three were her thoughts as she went.
A car braking hard at a tangent,
Could not quite avoid an accident.

The grocer weighs out potatoes
While we wait for the bell that echoes.
Her legs don't look right as she lies in repose,
Police and ambulance-men her bedfellows.

She lies beneath the hanging mistletoe,
A pound or more, not right at Xmas though.
Poor Mrs Burroughs.
Now try not to upset your mother so.

How cold: it feels like snow.
It was forecast on the radio.

SPECIAL SPECIES

THE HERON

The heron stands motionless
By reeds at the water's edge;
The air is heavy. There is silence.
Dark clouds gather and descend.
The lake becomes black and still.
Only the black clouds move, until
Sunlight flickers above far hills.
The lake's blackness intensifies.
Rain then falls, a silver curtain,
Each drop capturing the distant sun.
The lake coruscates, brief diamonds
Glitter, the cascade roars as if in rage
Against the indifference of the sky.
The clouds drift, sunlight intervenes.
The lake shines the reflected sky.
In the new surprising silence
An inevitable blackbird sings;
And the stoic heron dries his wings.

SWEET SLAVE

Hirundo, your life seems an endless flight,
Though bird thou ever art, sweet swallow,
Jewel of the air, blue and red and white.
Haplessly you are condemned to follow
Nature's implacable instructions, the code
Implanted in your mind, and heart, and soul,
Endless toil and danger is for you forbode
How do you reach your extraordinary goal?

Five thousand miles each way each season
Of your brief life, just three or four hard years.
For what purpose, what experimental reason
Incited the wild agency that made all our futures
Make some swallows wander, and others set
In static habitats, in pastoral peace and safety
While you and your kin were exiled and beset
By tempest, hunters, hunger, and no serenity.

Life's eyeless watchmaker did one good thing:
He gave you beauty: elegance and splendour.
And charming chatter too, though you can't sing.
But watching you in flight makes my heart tender.
How can happenstance create such wonder, why
Do love and pain together rule the swallows' nest?
The human mind may wonder, the soul may sigh,
But there's no consideration that will pass the test.

Bird and human, equally disposed to innocence,
Take their chance, do their dance, face the lance.
But swallow has its natural avian common sense:
While ten thousand miles is truly a great distance
And takes the bird two long months, there and back.
With four warm months in between for breeding
That leaves a holiday of half a year without lack
Of sunshine, socialising, and self-indulgent feeding.

TRIBES

A pride of lions.
A shoal of fish.
A skein of geese.
A herd of bison
A mission of monkeys
A swarm of locusts.
A patriarchy of humans?
Wherefore matriarchy?
A parade of elephants
A route of wolves
A mob of meerkats
A hive of bees
All these are inherently exclusive,
As are human tribes;
Needing their own:
Territory,
Language,
Laws,
Warriors,
Teachers,
Leaders . . .
And yet, exclusiveness kills and destroys
What it seeks to own;
It requires turning on its head,
Becoming inclusive, - of transcendent
Human values, universal values,
Overriding religion, gender, tradition, and
Everything else dividing our human beingness,
Rigid tribal loyalties no longer holding sway;
No need for violence and acts of terrorism
When fundamentalist agendas are overruled
And we are no longer caught in mindless fixity.

THE FROG CROAKED

Not his last, yet.
Spawn-work still,
Tiring. Repetitive.
'Then you croak',
He croaked. No fun.
The frog slept
Overwinter.
No fun, either.
Tree-rat thought
He knew his nuts
Well dug-in nearby
Hard digging
Time to rest
Where nuts?
Brushed his tail
Over the ground
No nuts around
Squirrel-woman
Beserked him:
Shouted 'Tree-sloth'
A scream unfair
He bit her.
Sparrow saw
Robin heard
Cat purred
Fur fled
A day for
Fight and light

THE TOAD SPAT

Larkin sulted
Poison skinned
Endangered
Is he happy?
Or merely sad
He's misunderstood,
A lazy toadstool-
Sitter he is not.
Energetic, though,
Not famously.
Handsome?
Some say not
Slow? That's
Sure. Rests
A lot, in
Compost, too.
Toadflax is
A pretty flower
Ivy-leaved
In your
Cellar, if
It can be
Lying low,
Clinging to
That wall
For dear
Life, insecure.
Toadgirl spawns

Amusement
All play no work
Makes Foxy fat
Not lazy
Only full of
Glorious sloth;
But Badger works
Dark and seriously.

A necklace:
Her masterpiece
What more
Is needed?
A mushroom
Would be
A nice change
To perch upon.

I PREFER INSECTS

Jewellery or jewelry, however you spell it
Jewelry is the only way to say it unless it
Makes you laugh to talk about Julery or it
Could even be Jew-ell-ery if you fancy foolery.

Precious or very-nearly-precious stones
May sound like semi-specious bones,
Parts of bands of underused skeletones,
Rattling a fatuous and predetermined drollery

Would you want to wear a tinny oxide, Cassiterite
Or Clinohumite, however rare, or Cat's Eye Scapolite,
A brooch of blood-red feldspar, Andesine Labradorite,
Or string your neck with Chrysoprase or a Chrysocolla?

Does the sound of Chrome Diopside produce a thrill?
And wouldn't gooseberry Grossularite make you feel ill?
Maybe a stick of Aragonic Ammolite could explode and kill?
While ghostly Goshenite is scary, and Howlite makes you weep.

Think instead, gem-lovers, of Jewel-Bugs, the Scutelleridae,
Those at least that shine and dazzle, metallic shields you see,
Red and green and not beetles, you cannot believe how pretty,
Although they smell a bit if prodded, just leave them happily to be.

Also alive and beautifully kicking are the Jewel Beetles, Buprestidae,
Epitomes of iridescence, green and intense, not bugs but beetley,
Proper Coleopts, with their elytra, where the colour is, and sweetly
They do fly, like our little ladybird, improbably, through the sky.

On a slow brook, near Mimulus, there hovers a flickering blue,
The Damsel-Fly, no Dragon this, a perfect predator it's true,
A diet of mosquitoes for this jewel of the stream, each time a new
Thrill of recognition, this damsel gives, this private, enchanted, view.

Butterflies are thrilling, jewels every one, white, brown or multihued
But of them all the blue are most ethereal, jewels of the first magnitude
Even the small wings of Common Blue, transform a garden's mood,
And seem to make the fearsome face of nature preposterously good.

So I prefer insects, alive and fragile; they are mortal, they are my kin,
I love them especially when they're beautiful, shining light within
The shadows of consciousness, where mere gemstones could not begin
To comfort or enliven, but make a dead chemistry of avaricious sin.

.

IN APPRECIATION OF CATS

Of the thousand cats I've known, only one was angry,
Constitutionally rather than spasmodically, innately,
Not reactively and justifiably, but yet understandably:
Living in an hotel in Aberdeen, what else could he be?

He sat upon a desk in the reception, a model of deception;
Affection seemed not to be within his limited perception,
My hand stretched out to stroke him, apparently a foul defection:
I think he would, uniquely, have attacked his own reflection.

Exception proves the feline rule: cats ingratiate or disappear
(Occasionally Cheshire-like) but most are happy to endear,
As lack of love, or supper, is what a cat is most disposed to fear,
And a surprising range of human sounds seems to please its ear.

But I confess to a mental block, and a history of interspecific shock:
Dogs and I are incompatible, the 'best friend' and I don't interlock.
Tongue-lolling, coprophagous, drooling, noisy, smellier than a sock,
Yet this snarling, dogged, biting, canine pest, struts like a turkey cock.

A cat may be moved to anger when its life or comforts are contested,
Or if its nightly wanderings, or its need for love, remain uninvested
With success, but a dog is angry by design, longing, raging, to be tested,
His appetites so barbarous he assumes a cat is put on earth to be ingested.

Odd as it may be, unlike cats, some dogs are made-to-measure slaves.
I almost admire their willingness to serve, the human spirit craves
To see woolly-minded sheep droved by cunning collies in tidy waves
And loves the placid ex-retriever when it the blind man on a zebra saves.

Therefore, in summary, praise to both creatures, with moderation;
Remember we are only human, not all capable of feline adoration.

ORANGES AND APPLES

The Orange was always the fruit of perfection;
While the Apple had sown the seed of defection,
Conspiring with Eve in committing the great sin
With the stealthy connivance of her sinuous twin:
The serpentine genius of evil temptation, Lillith.
The snake, in her coils of temptation, came with
Desire, lusting, tongue-tasting, encircling the tree
Bearing the sweetest of fruits, forbidden, yet free
For the taking, and the making of awakedness,
The knowing of life and of death and of nakedness.
Expelled from the garden, consumed with deep sadness
The lovers clung, hopeless, to the memory of gladness.
But to the patriarchs, in their pride and their power,
This alleged primal sin gave them joy hour by hour,
As they tortured and murdered in the name of deity:
They are ravenous beasts, for whom there's no satiety.
Into this ferment came Orange, a now rebellious fruit
Against infamous government, for they who refute:
Orange is the colour of discontent; if not always pure,
Yet it showed that humankind might still endure
And if Apple is knowledge and Orange is dissension
The two may still combine to make a new dimension.

OF ANGELS

And yet, here they are, in every guise imaginable, flawed;
And perfect, the sweetest of all the Jungian fruits, ambrosia
In everywoman's kitchen, custard and cream, ours to dream.

Human to the core, these angels, these only too mortals
No divinity in them but the godfulness of all and everything
On earth however bizarre or commonplace they may seem

Too obvious the girls and matrons in blue and stripy dresses
They are angels with grim or smiley faces, some even pretty,
Who wash and dose and feed the other angels in the scheme.

Patients are angels trying not to die, broken-winged, fallen
Innocently in nature's indifferent embrace, they wait, cry,
Grateful or enraged, suffering the pity of a merciless regime

And the hospital visitor colludes unwillingly in the drama
His own angelic nature in revolt or wet with angry tears
Caught in the crossfire, powerless, and needing to redeem

The mirage of the past, and make a garden of the future
Makes promises, plans, fine adjustments, angel on a pin,
Yearns to discover how to make truth and love supreme.

WOODLICE

The pink flagstones are neat,
And define the blue bellflowers
All washed white in the light
Of the bright full moon.
An orange rectangle
From an open door
Brings into sight
Woodlice in convocation.
Small one and larger ones
And all sizes in-between
Here free from the summer suns.
I stand and wonder:
Do they wrangle
When they visit this location?
Arriving with the evening showers
This, a mysterious focus
For crustaceans
So rarely seen
So far from the primordial sea.
Are these parliamentary seats
And is their leader
Facing some festival of doom
Originating in the ancient oceans?
Did the message pass through generations
The sacrificial part of tribal law?
Or perhaps an annual spree
For census of woodlouse populations
Within the garden's sphere?
Or is it some other ecstasy
Quite unrelated to fecundity.

POETRY, ART AND MUSIC

PROSPERO'S TANTRUM

If Prospero is not the old man of Zen's ox-herding fame
He's a ringer for the part, his island world a sandy void,
His life is nothing, and his long reign as a prestidigitator
As nullified as his nobility. A dissipated force, a nobody,
Like that old man wandering aimless in the market-place
After his dispossession by the cool, indifferent Void.
His enslaved spirit, Ariel, carries now the magic power,
In this un-tempestuous Tempest, perfunctory, ill-composed:
Irritating delinquents and an erupting goddess, Mother Ceres,
With even more than her usual pusillanimous irrelevance.
And Prospero's hissy fits are so petty and so self-important.
We are not, I warrant, meant to take him seriously at all.
Then to top it, after all the fuss about his fancy magic skills,
He just drops everything, pardons the homicidal maniacs,
And resolves to take up his old life as the provincial duke.
A worn-out playwright has his rights, we can't deny him them,
He was ready to exit left and who can blame him, like Prospero,
Except that William had earned a rest by a life of great invention.
Ariel and Caliban are wonderful ideas, though the others,
Including Prospero, are cardboard cut-outs or standard
Comic/drunken/delinquent stagey products of the time.
Perhaps Shakespeare was just tired of the average human
Being of Elizabethan times. After all, is our present culture
Replete with anything but the fundamental part of Shallow?

PROSPERO PARDONED

If I have any human right at all, it is to examine my own nature.
The Void is my dearest friend. And the most indifferent.
I can smell the freedom like salt in the wind from the North Sea.
I am Prospero in a revision of my 'Tempest' sitting on the sand
Outside my cell at the end of the events on this island.
Everyone has gone, except the half-human called Caliban.
I am alone. I am old and powerless. It is a good time to die;
Or go back to Milan, which is perhaps an even worse choice.
Why that thought, after twelve years longing for that City?
I hear the semblance of a voice. It is not my own.
Nor is it the growl of Caliban. It is sweet and tuneful.
What is it saying? I feel the presence of Ariel all around me.
But I can't understand what he is saying - or singing.
Or thinking. Can I understand my Ariel by ethereal osmosis.
It becomes clear to me that Ariel intends to stay with me.
Why that intention? How desperately he needed to be free.
But he is now free and he can choose my company.
Or not, as he sees fit. I speak into the salty air,
'My dear, why would you want time with me?
What can I give that you can't get for yourself?'
The word 'yourself' echoes in my head and then on,
And yet on again into sweet scented air around me.
How can it be that it is 'myself' that Ariel wants,
As a friend? Can a spirit have such ordinary ambition.
He seems not to hear my thought. There is silence.
Then Caliban comes lumbering awkwardly towards me.
Sideways, like a crab. Without preliminaries he says,

'I am sorry I wanted to kill you, Prospero. Ariel says
It was very stupid of me. I should have stood up to you.
If you want me to stay, there will have to be new rule.
Otherwise I am leaving. I can abide slavery no longer.'
'But where would you go. You're stuck here, are you not?'
'Never you mind what else I could do. Answer my question.'
'What was the question, Caliban? Tell it me again'
'Are you prepared to make new rules for the island?'
'Such as?' 'For example, that you and me are equals.'
'In what sense?' 'Don't be clever, Prospero. Every sense.'
'You'd want us to be partners, sharing duties,
Having joint ownership. That sort of arrangement?'
He nods his head vigorously. To my considerable surprise
This proposition is rather agreeable. I nod my head as well.
Ariel has come back and is hovering above me.
I feel both alone and in companionship.
I say to Caliban that I like what he requests.
'So you don't want me to leave, then?' he asks.
'No. But I'm still curious where you intended to go.'
'Ariel said he would get me away from here if I wanted.'
'And what did you tell him?' Caliban laughs softly,
A surprisingly pleasant sound, and replies,
'I told him I'd rather stay and that he found me a nice wife.'
'Sounds good, I wonder if he'd find one for me?'
'Now, then, Prospero, are you serious about all this?'
'Never more so,' I reply. I can see that my life
Might be just beginning. It could be too big a challenge.
But I have these two friends to help me through.
I will help them too. What a waste life is, otherwise.
'Will you write a play about us, Prospero?' And I reply:
'We will write a play together, all three of us, a true tale'.

SPECTRAL INITIATION

Eight hundred square inches of
White wood pulp, brilliantly blank,
Stare, vertical or flat, threatening
Un-cooperation, indifferent, as is
White's wont. It won't love me back
So dare I desecrate its virgin purity?
The teacher-man said, 'Remember, class,
This rectangle of nullity is all yours - do
Anything you like, just cover that bloody
Whiteness, it hurts your eyes'. Not true:
It hurts my pride; I cannot improve on
Perfect whiteness: I am white-bound.
I have colours: oily, plasticky, gouachey;
I have solvents, if no solutions, I have
Spirit, I have holy water, and detergent,
My armaments. I charge at the enemy
Gleaming whitely, insouciant, implacable
But mistaken, I have the force with me
Newton's stream of white is split by brush
And palette-scalpel, ROY G BIV emerges,
White fights back, holding on to territory
As the pigments gorge their way across
The untouched land, making things to make
The mystic realm bloom with desperation
So this is why the white was made to die?
To make this visual jabber, this potty pie?
You're all the same, artists, layabouts, wasters
Of the undefiled unconciousness, putting
Posters on holy walls, cartoons on monuments.
Gratified by graffiti, let the colours sing.

THREE PERSONAL CONFESSIONS

To The Wye
Scooter and Micky, in their sixteenth Spring, wanted a pilgrimage.
It was the hottest Good Friday ever and they needed running water.
On their bikes they did a hundred miles up and down the River Wye;
Defining themselves, defying family, returning burnt, ready for a bath.
Intellectual boys, full of science, poetry and music, their journey owed
Nothing to Easter celebration, it was a secular trip to internal Meccas.
They talked about free will, and sex, and politics, but never mentioned
Art, as such, because it would have been pretentious for growing boys.
Yet were full of it, unspoken, bound to science but in love with beauty,
They were unaware of all the art required for being happy by the Wye.

The Road to Uley
Before he was Scooter, a five-year old, he had known artistic ecstasy
In a handful of wild white violets, from the edge of an empty road.
Young enough to love uncritically; flowers, parents, sights and sounds.
His mind and heart were full of beauty even then, which never left him,
Yet he was in mid-life before he began another pilgrimage, an opening
Into the emptiness and silence of his inner being, seeking a connection
That could only be suspected, mystic and mysterious, as earth with sky.
As life with water, as in Uley's pools, from years and years before, love
And terror confronted him, strained within him, and, 'See us', they said.
So he saw, and drew pictures from his connection, his void, in his world.

Wild Orchids
Painting flowers, like people's faces, never arrived trustingly to him,
It was lazy and unauthentic, in his judgement, though he did it dutifully;
He felt disloyal because of orchids on the Hill, and the beauty of women,
It seemed like stealing something for himself, he wanted to give not take.
To give from his own consciousness, not borrow from another's life, fool
That he probably was, and still is, to disbar himself from artists' licence.
But he could please himself, protect the sanctity of the orchids and faces,
He earned his bread in the world and spent his talent on the easel, a deal,
If not made in heaven was, no product of hell. And now he's old, abstract
As his trees on paper, he can see hell in other painters' lives and works.

FOLDS OF EVOLUTION

1. The Lithics
A bad place to start, both then and now: how did they know what to do?
And how do we know what they were doing and how they were doing it?
The clues are few. Generally meaningless to modern mentalities. Stones,
Stones, and more stones. Then sophisticated images deep in caves. Holes.
Carvings. Ditches. Hills. Graves in abundance. Henges. Tools. Weapons.
Time is a mystery, at best, but worst in prehistory. Aborigines civilised
Australia fifty thousand years ago. Stonehenge was made in England
A mere five thousand years ago plus or minus another thousand or two.
How many human creatures made that world? How many kinds of human?
Imagine the number of people in London now, on a weekend, and imagine
That being the human population of the world some time in the Neolithic.
It was an ideal number, clearly, to have achieved so much so cheaply,
Even though it took a long time. How long exactly is only to be guessed.
So were they all artists, or was someone catching and cooking lunch?

The arithmetic is unimportant. The great issue is the art. Considering
Everything, humankind has never been so aesthetically productive since.
For all the effort and the quantity, the quality hasn't been maintained.
As in everything except making babies and killing all else, humans
Have lost our evolutionary momentum, which is interesting but not
As important as why they did so well when they were primitive nobodys.
Some answers suggest themselves. To be as good at art as they were
The Lithics must have had some astonishing inspiration. From somewhere.
How? And What? I ask again. Shamans, yes, but how did they come in?
Our brains are now so addled by wordiness, of gods, ego and knowing,
It is left to free agnostics to accept the mystery to be mystical, oddly
Embracing what clerisy denies, that goddiness exists in this godless world.
So the god is in the art, art is in the god, as the Lithics came and went
And stones on stones and animals on walls from and to the Void was sent?

2. Riot of Reification

In the beginning was the wordless, then the heavens broke. Gods rained,
Gods reigned, Abrahamic madness gushed like a geyser in the wasteland
Once the master, art became servile and disempowered, an implement;
Of clerical manipulation, an early dumbing down, of the mystical urge.
Occidentally it was in a reprocessed volcano god, Yaweh, Jehova, whatever.
Orientally, at first god-free, but soon infected, an eastern oxymoron called
Buddhism; and a secular kindness called Tao. But art still suffered. Why? How?
Buddha was a pragmatic mystic, his image became the art, fat and smiling,
Gold and graven, while paintings sank into soggy landscapes, rose in foggy
Mountains, bamboo leaves lolled uneasily beneath a crest of snow. Peace
Hovered anxiously, suffering lurked in the heart, unseen, art died in China.
In the middle flourished families of gods, dressed up animals, mad humans
Walt Disney could have designed the sets and characters, such was the 'art'
Of Egypt, Greece, Rome, and India, in the bright glare of those dark ages.

Abraham, meanwhile, and his endless progeny, made a universe of art. Big
God pictures: saints, sinners, torn flesh, hanging corpses, weeping women.
Suffering made virtuous, human evil expiated by death of sons, blood ran,
Everywhere, bodies burnt alive, this was art of the dreadful, weirdly vacuous.
Elsewhere, at times, were big biceps and minute penises, throbbing breasts,
Breathtaking nymphs and satyrs in Bacchanalia, lumpy statues to horny gods.
Churches stuffed with jewels and erotica, clerics like fashion models, operas
Of love and loss, monarchs pious and homicidal, and the art of the hideous
Thrived for centuries, as if humankind had given up, as if stunned by war
And worship, living in kitsch, millions of crucifixions, the dross of crosses,
And lovely, mindless virgins with fat children. Or a 'Garden of Delights';
Sinister, risible, beautiful and scatological, the art of sadomasochism, how
Hieronymus was he? And Leonardo ruled with Michelangelo, Latin lovers,
An uncivil partnership made in Neverland, lotuses in a heavenly swamp.

3. Reflection

Sixteen hundred to nineteen hundred, ran the tide, trying, wearily,
To turn itself, to find truth and beauty, an art free from sin and gods.
But clerics merely morphed into princes, they who now ruled a newly
Half-secular existence. Artists were still slaves whatever their rebellion.
As if Bach had given way to Beethoven, as he had, but visually, seeing
A world of nature and creatures afresh, the creative mind opening. Yet
Hounded by old fantasies, dead dogmas, not so old, not so dead, still
Growling, and still sugary sweet in hypocritical cups, in silver spoons.
It was a turbulent shore on which to see the great ocean of possibility.
Was there a visual Beethoven in those four centuries? Did art wake up?
Maybe Degas, perhaps Gauguin, Van Gogh certainly, of course Goya,
Manet too, Matisse barely, Monet maybe, Rembrandt just squeezed in, early,
Renoir, I guess, Seurat surely, Turner too, and Velazquez simmers well.
On reflection, these twelve pioneers gave the beginning of an optimism.

4. Dystopia

And some lingers, in Picasso, Mondrian, Modigliani, and even Schiele;
Klee and Miro have fun, Kandinsky plays abstractly, Hockney havers,
Bacon fries the mind, but the rest is froth and futility: with one immense
Exception, the mighty Rothko, the only one to tell the swooping mind
To face itself and swim in the swell of emotion, abstract but passionate.
With his death the optimism also died. Lunacy gained dominance. Even
If some still reach for beauty and truth, fashion and finance prevail.
The inanity of 'performance art' invades the culture, and a dirty bed is
Exhibited, foul objects displayed, and the farcical 'artist' gets famous as if
Grubbiness was thrilling, and another weirdo puts sharks and cows in
Tanks of formaldehyde, or offers a diamond encrusted skull and paints
Rudimentary pictures as bad as the bed-maker's. Is it intended that art
Should be so defiled as to make anything sell? Is this the drug mentality?
Rothko ended his life in time, he'd have so suffered in this ruined world.

AND NOW IMPLACABILITY

Chronic karma comes and goes around, circling in our heads and bones.
Those long, exhausting, Lithic battles with the mystery still not won:
Stonehenge stands in witness while we, witless, make a pickled shark
That grins our love and hate for nature, and mimics our imprisonment.
But bloodied nature still stands, gesticulating its pain and enslavement,
We show it to ourselves, gloating in our power, weeping in our grief;
In a million works of art, mirrors of our grandiosity, as our Rome burns.
Or is it the twilight of our ungods, have we invented evil to consume
Ourselves as we have consumed the earth, has art dwindled down to this?
Put the pictures end to end and see the miles of human hubris stretch away
Into an unknown future from an unknown past, and it tells all our lies.
This line of falsehood is not infinite: we came, we have not conquered,
And we must go. Nature will spit us out, and we do not have the art
To encompass that expulsion, nor do we believe it, we who are the world.

Could art be the saviour of our skins? We have tried god and science
And they have failed us, and we them, but is there something still to do?
If we have any value, in any way, at all, what good could we bring
To this suffering world? Nature is the cradle of our being, we are its child.
We may recognise how badly we have behaved, our art shows us how.
But somewhere in our inner depths there may be a dormant promise.
Could we, even now, begin the belated growing to some maturity?
Obviously improbable, given the evidence of our own eyes, that's true.
But nature, the great continuity, will not give us much more grace.
We shall suffer an expulsion, no doubt, and some of us may be around
To record the blood-fest in a sort of art, only nearly all is lost to physics
As energy itself is never lost, merely its form, the form of nature;
Can we change our being to accommodate reality, must we fantasise?
Time will tell and art may record its telling, or maybe, sadly, not.

WHAT IS ART?

What is art? An artifice?A truthfulness?An essence?
All these. But also an act of transcendence demanding
Superb endeavour, great skills, a magic touch, a muse
Perhaps, or an imminent, brave, and wonderful daemon
Demanding unique expression, absolute dedication, not
Merely decoration on a wall, wise saying on the page, not
Sweet melodies, a perfect harmony, these may be a music
Enough in itself, but not enough to change the human mind.

Hear a Beethoven concerto, through the mind and body of
A Brendel, a Richter, or any of the many musical sorcerers and
The virtuoso joy flows upon our ears and souls: astonishment
And love and ecstasy. That is transcendence and it is sacred.
Here is the true spirit of humanity, beyond us, within us, as if
A Paganini or a Caruso or a Rembrandt arise as mutant beings
Showing us the limit of our nature, the upper reach of ourselves.
These are gods, or archetypes, tokens of possible perfection.

The arts of painting, swimming, sailing, dancing, teaching, seeing
Speaking, cooking, acting, loving, running, helping, caring, living:
All have famous names, fame that means more than recognition,
The measure is achievement, a grace, an ease of expression, and
Not just good, not just superb, not just supreme, but an act of being;
An ineffability that arise from within the creative act, mysterious, and
Arcane. This is The Art, and it grows from the quality of being, so that
It mirrors the soul and is itself an endless celebration of our existence.

THOMAS PUSILLANIMOUS

There is the book, made by Phoenix,
In the two thousandth year of myth
Of one particular god, or two, maybe
Out of the many thousands of their kind.
Thomas chose his duogod or it chose him.
Universalists imagine only one, Thomas
Seemed to also, but it bothered him to death.
In more than five hundred poems. I read on,
And on, and on. At first the obsessions and
Pretensions made the works too sour to taste
Let alone enjoy. What daemon drove him?
Well, this ghastly god of his, monotonously.
Some men need a god, some men don't: R.S.
Couldn't bear his own allegiance, so why
Not put it in the bin? It kills the poetry for me.
Serial obsessive they call him now, well; yes.
Still I persisted and found one and twenty
That appealed. That is four per cent, I know.
So ninety-six per cent of his life's work left me
Cold? It did. And not just god. The man himself
Lurked abominably behind almost every line.
Focus on the few, then. There was that little list:
I suppose one may forgive a clergyman his god
Obsession; even forgive a clergyman for being
A clergyman. But these direful poems make me
Grateful for the sublime existence of a Larkin's
Wit. It is astonishing to think Thomas nearly
Made a Nobel. A joke it must be. Pull the other
Leg. If Wales needs a poet, I would far prefer
That other Thomas: drunken, flamboyant,
Dylan, bless his holey cotton socks.

THREE POEMS OF HOMAGE

1. William Wandering As A Lonely Cloud

In the cold light of morning I saw I was lost at last, unready as I was for it.
An insistent dream of wandering had challenged me to receive my saving grace.
Exciting and unendurable, vacuously racing through villages, cities, scary space,
With no return to friendship and home. I stormily refused eternal exile, fleet
In my own carelessness, running on ahead, streets and hills drawing my feet
Until I stopped at a tourist shop and asked if I could buy a map, a last resort.
The lady smiled, saying she'd seen the pain in my eyes and knew I was past
All help but hers and the maps were not much use being of somewhere else
So there was nothing to be done and she would see my sufferance would last.

2. Thomas Eating Peaches, Counting Coffee Spoons

In the blight of solitude, no bliss, where body against soul, spirit versus mind,
Those old antonyms, used to rule now finished. New monarchs, magnetic poles,
Have taken over, un-metaphysical lords, come and go, make and break and lose.
My needs are false and true. I want the desire for itself and reject it when it holds
Me too tight, and I breathe and choke, and life becomes too easy and too difficult.
I need to trust, I do not trust, trust me, do not trust me. Trust divides me from
Myself, distrust holds me together, and I and you are too old and too young
Too sweet, too sour. I taste myself with distaste, I lick my salty skin, eyeing
Wrinkles and grey strands, denying aged callowness with infantile infinite wisdom.

3. Philip In The Hole Of Life: Treasure Trove

I am there in spirit, even soul I suppose, on this planetary paper, here and there
For you, for me, in our enduring crisis. I cannot live for you or you for me, for
Two, whatever the song says, cannot live as one nor without either, nor even I
For me, or you for thee, whoever you may be, everyman and every lady before
His and her unmade maker. What is the crisis? I hear the indifferent chorus chant:
Greeks in love with rhetoric and mystery, though killing questioners on principle;
Romans enjoying our disembowelment in the grateful dust; Augustinian cant
Surfing the centuries until the Cartesian virus and Newtonian cooking apples
Brought us to divine doubt; yes, what crisis is it that merely eats uncertainty?

MUSIC MAGI

The magi of song and dance give freely to the hungry soul
Reverberations from the ever-fertile Void, a benevolence
That spread in space and time; since consciousness began.
Music has the most intimate power in the human mind,
Direct and universal, a cornucopia of emotional inception
Musical expression; a gigantic evolutionary panorama,
Nevertheless has not been given its full credit by our kind.
No muse has ever been more ill-used, no glory so denied.
As if great Mozart and shining Schubert had never been on earth
Music may languish as entertainment or accompaniment to food
A practice that diminishes both the greater and the smaller art.
Worst of all is how it is made to drag and squall irrelevantly
To dramatize and trivialise, distracting, drowning information.
Worse still, its prostitution to the violence of military automatons,
And its caricature in the raucous howl of bagpipes and brass band.
Dreariest of all, poor music dribbled meaninglessly into bars and lifts.
Punks young and old shout and gesticulate on stroboscopic stages;
Crooners smirk and slurp for Christmas and for sugar-sweet erotics;
Manic pianists plonk and stomp for drunken revellers, what jazz!;
Dancers smooch and hop and wriggle, a mockery of animation;
And classical copyists incentivise like throbbing casino wheels.
No muse has ever been more ill-treated. But it matters very little.

Music can overcome the contortions it is persuaded to perform.
It is pure bodhisattva. It come out of the Void and saves our souls.
How blessed we are, a species raised in the infinite glory of music.
Music reminds, anecdotally, of a hackneyed epigram of biology:
The perpetual, natural, Recapitulation of Phylogeny by Ontogeny,
How every human foetus is fish then frog then reptile then mammal.
In that development, as mind appears, rhythmic sounds attend,
Sounds from mother, before and after birth, and then the sound around,
Euphony and cacophony, all processed through the mental mixer,
Mill-grist for every musical magician, whether genius or facile fixer.

AN DIE MUSIK

A flaxen-headed choirboy, I was set to please,
Yearning, archetypal, yet somehow ill at ease,
Sang carols cold on doorsteps, spirit full a thrill,
Mystical compulsion filling my embryonic will.

Then that dream died, still uneasy as in its life
And lay unquiet in its grave, regretful shadows rife:
Broken voice, now, broken hopes, no longer winging.
But, hiding my unease, new hope to me came singing

Concertos, symphonies, and string quartets disposed
Love upon me, and they my all too human voice deposed
Now were the years of listening, discovering, and learning
That subdued, or pacified, the voice's everlasting yearning.

Two musics in my ear, one of strings, or brass or wind of wood
The other crooning casanovas, sweet jezebels, bad or good,
Until I walked the winter journeys of a German baritone:
Dietrich Fischer-Dieskau hustling me upon the gramophone

Not yet, not yet, my musical epiphany had to wait
Until I was nearly old, when it was certainly too late
To become an English baritone however hard they'd try
To resurrect the dormant youth and teach him how to fly.

A few years of daily grind took me to the edge of competence,
And singing to an audience was rather more than mere pretence.
For a time I lived that choirboy's dream, tone by joyful tone,
But there was another ringing in my head, a frantic telephone.

I had learned the way to sing, but wasn't it an empty shout?
This performance was just old egotism putting its ugly self about.
Could a singer tell a story without the need for sweet applause?
Wasn't it the moment to reconsider, to take a pregnant pause?

So, at last, I did. It was a dramatic, if not tragic, confrontation.
The shaky treble of the child seemed to echo in my concentration.
This was not the way to end, with Schubert's Will-'o-the Wisp,
I had some life to live before my conversion into a potato crisp.

LAND AND WATER

BEAUTIFUL EARTH

Green, and blue, and white; an orb in space
A planet governed by us, the human race,
Who have waste-landed this environment
Without sense, nor love, nor even just discernment
And now we live in a still lovely chaotic land
But catastrophe advances across the barren sand.
We believed ourselves to be masterly and brilliant
Even looking greedily out to the uninhabited firmament
As if easier than putting right the wrongs on earth.
How slow we are to realise how little we are worth

THE DAY OF THE RIP

And nearly R.I.P. for me upon that shining day
A Near Death Experience, as some are wont to say.
My eighteenth summer: free at last, and by the sea
Seen once before, across a mile of mud, and hardly
Identifiable as ocean, down in Weston-super-Mare.
Far west I'd come now, through Cymru, to where
Land ran out into the sand of Marloes, Westdale Bay,
Beyond reddish cliffs, half a billion years old, some say
Immensity of cobalt sea, at Little England Beyond Wales
Looks so placid, last things in my mind are coffin nails;
Though I know I am a clumsy novice, I can't resist the charm:
Leaving that torrid beach behind, it can surely do no harm?
Walk into the gentle waves and a short experimental swim?
Keep away from jagged rocks, they are exceptionally grim,
But ahead an endless rippling swimming pool is lying
I am strong and young and can do it without trying.
A life-time later, five minutes of ordinary time awareness
I turn to look to shore and maybe wave, the friends I bless,
But there is only emptiness, as if they never were, then I see
Little figures on a slender line, far away, too far to see me.
I drop my feet to stand on solid sand, but there is only sea
Beneath me, then I feel the current around my body, coldly
Uncalculatingly carrying my foolish self out to mid-Atlantic
And I realise that I am near my end because of this crazy antic.

It would be something of an understatement to say I am terrified
And an exaggeration to confess that I am completely mystified
Where did I go wrong, for certain I was only gently splashing,
But I am still hurtling to oceanic outer space, my life is flashing
Before my half-blinded eyes, and I would quite prefer to live.
Yet I am being forced along towards an everlasting mighty sieve.
Then, an odd conception: those jagged rocks way over to my right;
Could I go sideways, escape the lethal grasp, keeping them in sight.
Frantic flailing with legs and arms, last gasp, lost hope, nearly dead,
I am actually moving, towards the projecting teeth of rock ahead.
I float a while to recover energy, than I go on again. I am half asleep
Then woken, moments or hours, later by piercing pain: I must keep
Calm, come to my senses, which I do, and see that I am merely impaled
Upon the friendly rocks, not sorry that the mendacious sea has failed.
Bloodily I crawl towards the sands, and there I suffer yet another blow
My fellow-students are not surprised to see me, not having seen me go.

PLANT PLANET

The humans, last to arrive, just lately come
Upon the plants' planetary domain, home
Of phytogenesis long, long, before animal
Snout arrived and that, millennia times millennia,
Preceded Johnny-come-lately, early man.
But still, the nouveau invader learned at last
That plants were primary creators of life. from
Whom great blessings flowed, the holiest of grails.
And so man made plants holier still, made them gods
Or companions, or ends, of gods. Such as Odin, Wotan
Of the North, hung to mature upon a branch of Yggdrasil
The cosmic ash-tree, and that Egyptian victim of fratricide
Osiris, enclosed in a coffer in a Tamarisk tree, or Buddha,
Finding his transcendence beneath the bodhi tree, or Jesus
The Jewish messiah, slaughtered upon a cross of wood;
Or sundry Siberian shamans taking up positions in holy trees.
And then the lotus, rising from the mud,
To bear the god in a cup of leaves.

Meanwhile the growing herd of humankind
Existentially broke free from normal beastly ways,
The foraging, the hunting, the reverential catching
As catch could in the jungle, on the plains,
And even in the trees and waters of the earth,
Passed into history and the first great revolution:
Farming was born; mankind became the owners of the world.
Like warfare, farming is pure hubris: power ran wild in the land
And in a millennium or two, the scattered thousands became
Billions, lurching chaotically and inevitably towards starvation.
Greed and incompetence stalked the land,
Tearing the soil from hills, making floods, or deserts,
For food, or fuel.Or just for territory.
The rape is the same, regardless of purpose,
And the worst death is the killing of the trees,
As they are killed, ultimately mankind kills itself
And we shall all die in the mud or the sand
Of the plant planet's murdered land

LOWER LITTORAL ROUNDUP

If your life is on the edge, or in extremity, emigrate to the seashore,
Especially if you're small, a little slow, and bothered by enmity.
So consider the lower littoral, zone of low tides, usually very wet.
A sanctuary of stability, where seaweeds bloom, zoological diversity.
Why would any creature ever leave it? Possibly from boredom?
Admittedly it's crowded, a lot of riffraff, and no border controls.
You would be among companions who like moderation, who hate
To be dry, abhor the cold and dislike it hot, but a motley lot at best.
Diversely boring, though individually amusing, it is a generous slice
Of nature, crowded into a narrow strip mostly tided over by the sea.

It's a garden, wracked with seaweeds, brown and green and red,
Rooted to the rocks or rising flamboyantly from their marine bed,
From a holdfast; the thallus waves above, stipe and blade reach out,
This Fucus or that Ascophyllum, maybe a gentle green Cladophora.
Like plants of land, the lovely Algae are called weeds by an animal,
Homo supremo, for whom a weed is any plant not in the right place.
Or used ignominiously for food, or fertiliser, or herbal medicine.
Animals are culled, plants are harvested, by human super-predator:
When he comes hunting, the sanctuary is violated, the sea-garden
Is ploughed down, diversity destroyed, and boredom a lost luxury.

Littoraly a subterranean animal reserve, safe from big predators,
Like fish, but not new big predators such as the likes of you and me.
No backbones, these beasts, but none the worse for that, so diverse,
Full of surprises, wonders, amazements, how do they do it, and why?
Because they're there, the gastropods, the molluscs, the crustaceans,
The hydras, the anemones, the sponges and the worms in tubes, they're
In the web of life just like the rest of us, and getting on with it, quietly.
Some are pretty, and pretty strange, like the nudibranchs, sea slugs, all
Colours of the spectrum, all shapes and sizes. Consider other molluscs:
Abalone, ormer, chiton, mussel, limpet, sea-snail, and endangered whelk.

And crustacean marvels, the crab, the shrimp, and the water woodlouse,
The mollusc and the crustacean invented suits of armour before backbone
Became the inner solid being, a change if not a clear improvement, if
Soft on the outside is a bad idea. But these armour-plated creatures have
A distant relative, the echinoderm: sea urchin, starfish or sea cucumber,
The spiny-skinned ones, radially symmetrical, and living only in the sea.
Ten different kinds of worm make tubes to live in, and some are showy,
Like the Feather Duster Worm. But the weirdest of the little water beasts
Is the sponge, no nerves, no gut, no circulation, it just lives with the flow.
Lastly is the sea anemone, beautiful and vicious, the killer in the shallows.

A DAY DAWNED

A day dawned golden, when I knew I was a river, not a road.
As when a child I had dreamed and lived a country stream,
Before my youth set out upon a path bearing the futile load
Of mere ambition, leaping banks, crossing bridges, eyes agleam.
Not a road then, nor following a path, except the ways to hills
And down again, through valleys, to have the company of brooks
Was to be within the water, the water within me, such childhood
Required and was given in and of the nature in which I wild-lived.

Once lost, my river-self drowned in dryness, as if a soul parched,
Full-human in my hubris, travelling upon the earth, my river-being
Trapped in aridity of canals, dead water, or locked in traffic jams;
I was now man, a maker of blank miracles, no longer inner-seeing.
Not that I knew myself lost. The beacons blazed bold promises,
I was on the road to everywhere, clear in the achievement-brochure
There were no dragons, no minotaurs raged, I ached with destiny.
And the river I had been was dammed, blasted, silted, and abandoned.

How, then, has this golden vision shone through, anew, on this day?
It has been thirty summers and thirty winters, to make the void and
Then make it full, a sweet space, for my stream-self to flow again,
For bridges and manufactured waterways to fall and fail, the roads
And rails to pit and break, the green of travel wither, the high life
To lie low, a generation, to joyous catastrophe: the bells rang loud
In my creaking skull, they slowly made me wake. I knew them,
Though not their meaning, and the understanding came near late.

To live a river is to stand, still, in time, yet move molecularly, enigma
Unknown to life as road, which lies low and lets the world go by,
A busy nonentity, as was I, before I became a stream again. Moving
As a rivulet or brook, I stay within my world and it moves with me
I am a continuity within continuity, everything is congruent with all.
Nothing has changed, everything has changed, I am a rural beck again,
I harbour little fishes and water crowfoot, kingcups on my shoulders,
A kingfisher shines bright above me; I watch the tadpoles grow feet.

THE HAND AND GUT OF MAN

I stood at Drakestone Point, up on the mighty hill,
Looking at the silver Severn writhing across its plain,
Wild orchids at my feet, freedom flowing in the air:
Here was joy, and mystery, above the great river there,
Five miles distant, five miles near, and two miles wide.
That was a lifetime past. Now stands foul old Magnox
In the centre of the view, dead but toxic, all power spent,
Still decades away from being innocent again, if ever,
For ingenious minds intend to bury radioactive waste
In that rotting hulk, from other Severn power stations,
Thus we treat our rivers, mere sewers and conveniences,
Or playthings, like the hill, handed to the mad god, Golf.

If origins mean anything, Severn is a Celtic river, rising
Near the Irish Sea upon the slopes of a Welsh Mountain,
And fifty bridges and crossings are in the Land of Cymri.
The hand of man has been laid heavily upon the Severn
In England, obsessively in Shrewsbury and Gloucester,
And mightily between Wales and England, no-one asked
The River, no consultation of riparian oracles, not even
The Great Gods, Golf and Greed. Nor of tributary deities,
Generous Vyrnwy, Tern, Teme, the Avons, Wye, and Usk.
No fish-spirits, if they existed, were asked if they minded
The massacres of salmon and eel, the harvested elvers
Guzzled in billions to near extinction, by the gut of man.

The Severn rises tempestuously, in an eight foot wave,
Rushing faster than the feet of man, a bore against a bore.

HILL AND VALLEY

My father's gift
To his young bride
Was a new house
Halfway up a hill
Steep on a main
Road going on
Towards the sea.
Her house backed
To walled garden
Then to vertical pasture
And in summer
Endless blue scabious.

As I was very small
On hands and knees
Going through the wall
By a two foot door
Green with brown bolt.
Often escaping I went
To the top of the hill
No dog required
No-one ever met
I left the mad sealyham
Sheep-chasing Fury
But time were safer then

Up the sharp tilted hill
To the ridge-backed crest
With wild earthen track
Plunging past farmhouse
And on to the deep valley
Named Sychpant, quiet
Secluded, peace, placid
Stream, stopping place.
Looking up ahead, high,
Mountain, path goes on
Where legions marched
And died and lay buried

A stone monument there
Marked my limit then.
And now I see my path
Is a line of continuity

PARADISE ROAD

I was born in paradise, though some would call it Bloody Dursley,
And Paradise Road went round in a circle, from Uley's big Bury
All the way to Wotton-Under-Edge, with hills and streams within.
I spent my youthful years finding a way out, the new life to begin.
The road I lived on was called First Avenue, no way out of there
There was a little factory at the end making energy machines where
My father spent his life painting them green, but green was all around:
In trees and fields and ponds and gardens and each everlasting mound.
Literally north, metaphorically mental, and actually, to Birmingham,
The road I travelled, breaking out, sadly, though I didn't give a damn.
Homesick for hills and kin, I had at last made my first great big mistake.
The idea was to keep on going for the greater paradise, some big break,
The god of science beckoned, along that golden paving, some sublime,
Some divine, good fortune, why not me? It could have been my time.

That road went underneath the Rubicon of my mind and I didn't notice
Upon my wounds and growing pains I spread a nicotine-and-ego poultice
Eight years I stumbled on, acquiring my credentials, the route obscure
As Jude's and no more sure. Then 'Up the Great North Road', to endure
An error of greatest magnitude yet, Yorkshire Farmers, Yorkshire Fog,
No leylines here, no blooming orchids, just a noisy road to Askham Bog.
It was then a suspicion grew, a tadpole in my murky mind: was I wrong?
Had I misread the road-signs that seemed to hold a promise in their song?
I revisited Paradise Road, found it gone, and the energy machine was dead.
No retreat to the prison I'd escaped, all dead, but no obsequies were said.
No avenue of retreat, no sunlit path to the horizon, the dream was gone
And still I hadn't found it. 'Keep going', said I to me, as to an only son;
'You just haven't looked hard enough, it must be there somewhere, go on,
Walk the talk, cake the walk, there's the road, behind the hill, and so on.'

It took some time for penny's bad fall, sometime before time I called:
Last orders and several for the road. It was late, I was nigh on appalled:
Forty years had drained away, I was nearly old. I walked the woodland,
On paths through myself, old paradise paths that still dappled, good land
Within, still waiting, where the myths of progress smelled like ramsons,
My ransomed essence found me again, and no need to blow ram's horns.
I had not needed to walk that road, that adventurous way, had I known
A truth that waited for me to find it. Not too late. I have it deeply sown.
What is it? That 'Overwhelming question'? That overwhelming answer.
That the myth of progress fattens on the truth of being, fools the chancer:
There's no outer road to anywhere that matters more than here. I walk to
To where I already am; there is no path, no road, nor even easy avenue.
If I meet myself unawares and find myself in every conscious meeting
I will not care that life is short, and I'm glad that everything is fleeting.

THE WAY TO WATERLEY BOTTOM

Now I will never know. I tried too late. Did not ask.
She spoke with passion. Rare passion for her. Anger
Was her passion. Usually. But this was love, or beauty.
I did listen. Did I believe? I did believe. But not enough.
It was the loveliest place she'd ever seen. Oh the flowers!
At last I went to look. What took me so long? To try it?
She said it was a hard walk. Up the escarpment vertically
Then down the other side, vertically. She told me the name.
Breakheart Hill. Said with her usual grim satisfaction. Doubt
Gripped me: she was not good on her legs; could she have
Climbed Breakheart, after rheumatic fever, on poor legs?
I was young and strong then and did not doubt myself
The way I doubted her, and said, 'Mum, I'm off to Breakheart,
See you later.' She said nothing, just her usual sad smile.
I got halfway, and thought about it, hard, it wasn't halfway:
I'd only reached the summit, to which I'd have to return,
Hours later, I supposed. Bored rather than tired, this Nature
Mystic was tired of trees and falling over, athletic as I was.
This was a fool's errand, a wild goose chase, I was too young
To be patient. I chased back down the hill and then wandered
Slowly home. I told her she was right. She knew that already.

Had she set a trap? The humiliation of the hubritic brat? She
Was capable of that, love me though she might. So I failed her
And myself. Then thirty years passed and she was dead and I
Still had not seen Waterley Bottom in full flower. But had she?
Maybe, they walked everywhere then, when she was ten, or twenty.
And now I had a company car and need not negotiate Breakheart.
I took the low road from Tyndale's monument, on Nibley Knoll,
Looking for my mother's dream. And found it. Breakheart, evaded
Literally, still struck me down, sitting in the driver's seat, I looked
Upon the scruffy backwater, flowerless, a metaphorical lost hope.
Was it lovely when the young Hilda saw it? Yes it must have been,
She spoke with passion. But I was too late, and would never know.

PATH OF PROFANITY

Watch the language: myths of road and path and time:
They move not, a road goes nowhere, a path stays still,
Time itself is static: while people walk along them all.
Word is that Avebury was made five thousand years ago
And it's a mystery as to who erected the hundred stones.
A temple or a killing place, who knows, and why the hill?
Silbury, and other things, the Avenue, the Kennet Barrow,
An immensity of concept, a magnificence of creation, and:
A road runs through it, a modern slab of tarmac profanes
The Pagan place and a village with its church squats there
Where centuries of collective vandalism and puritanical
Zeal have not quite succeeded in a complete eradication.
Yet the road does not run, and nor does time, they stand,
And where is the profanity and what is sacred on this land?
They meant to fight the devil as they smashed the stones,
Standing in their time, knowing no other way, no road
To take them to or fro, fixed minds, fixed time, fixed space.
Now sweet tourism plays its tune, come play in Avebury;
Cars and coaches career upon the anachronistic road. Hear,
Crows calling in the hedonistic air, here is absolutely now.
What then is the continuity? What is it that moves? Where
Was then if nowhere? Where is tomorrow if it cannot come?
A hundred stones for eternity, or a day, there is no certainty
As roads and avenues are equivocal, no going, no coming.
Forget meaning, forget purpose, and see the face of freedom
In the Avebury stone circle, the karmic roundabout, a home.
Let prophets have their moment then snuff them out, they know
Nothing, nor do we, leave time to itself, it won't go away. Take
No road for none leads anywhere but back to you. Stay on your
Chosen path, walk it, then move off when you've had enough.

HOUSE AND HOME

HOUSES/HOMES

Houses are not necessarily homes
They can also be prisons
If you do not live up to, or fulfil,
Family dreams or expectations.
Homes are places for safety:
The other night we saw a programme,
'Places of Safety', rabbit-burrows, badger setts,
And holes excavated by water-voles.
The badgers were rescued orphans
Five had already bonded into a group
The sixth, a female, small and vulnerable
And out in the world could she survive alone?
A human observation
Of an animal situation
That was too much like
A common human tragedy.
Why was the sixth orphan badger
Unacceptable?
Was she too young, too weak; a liability to the rest?
Human compassion often, if not always,
Tries and sometimes succeeds
In redressing apparent imbalance
If nature otherwise fails to notice
Or deliberately ignores
A special need for housing care,
Has human consciousness moved on
Or is it just fooling itself?

THE CASTLE

In a place of birth though not of pleasure
Where I knew that I was not a treasure,
And only my achievement was the measure,
I couldn't hope to live up to expectation.
But there was a golden place of delectation
That released my being from affectation.
It was the place of my grandmother's home
Where a lonely eight-year-old could roam
Beyond the green, towards the estuarine foam.
I often walked alone along the golden sand,
Until I came upon the entrance to the hidden land.

There was the narrow lane, willow-herb each side,
Until steep concrete steps climbed up towards a ride,
A grassy path that took me through the dark beech wood
To a sunny dell, where I listened to the silence as I stood
Encircled and protected by the pillars of the trees.
Then the songs of birds sweet enough to please
My lonely heart, in the radiance through purple leaves.
At the end of the wood, the emerald bracken weaves
Around a gate that opens on to a flowering field
That rises gradually until there stands revealed
In broken omnipotence, neglected and alone
The old gigantic castle made of weathered stone

My empty castle, unvisited except by me, so long ago,
Yet full of its own past, into which my life can flow;
And like a karmic cycle the staircase of broken power
Spirals up against the wall inside the crumbling tower.
My childish hubris finds a way to climb from stone to stone
Too young for vertigo, temptation strong, all fear flown:
Through the broken banisters I get glimpses of the floor
Far below. I press my back upon the wall and so ensure
I do not fall; I see the landscape through the arrow slits
The way of my return. But into my new awareness flits
The knowing that this is my place for ever, this tower,
A refuge for my spirit so that it and I need never cower.

HOME THOUGHTS OF A BOY

This is my home, though my parents think it's theirs.
I live in the Front Room when I have it to myself;
Mum lives in the Kitchen. Dad lives in the Garden
Or at Work. Till evening, when they're in with me.

My house was put up for me in 1931 when I was born.
It's made of pebble-dash, tiles, metal window frames,
Three bedrooms, inside lavatory, bathroom, pantry,
My front room, Mum's kitchen, and Dad's big garden.

Mum is always polishing. So my front room shines
And smells nice. There's a table, a sideboard, settee
Easy chairs, red-tiled fireplace, cupboards, pictures,
(Me on the sideboard), Dad's gramophone on a table.

In the Winter we play cards and eat toast by the fire
Dad gets a wireless which needs an accumulator,
And we listen to Plays and the News. In Summer
I go fishing and pick mushrooms and strawberries.

I get primroses and bluebells in Spring and Mum
Puts them in vases on the table in my Front Room.
She gets me books and I keep them for the Winter.
There's a newspaper but I don't read it. Just my books.

At the front there's grass and borders with flowers,
Mum's Lilies-of-the-Valley, grow under the window.
There are lupins and delphiniums at the back, near Dad's
Shed. The garden is also full of vegetables and salad plants.

My Aunty buys me a little bike and I ride up and down
In the road outside my house. There's a photo of me on it
Looking happy for Aunty. I have a gang as well. We hunt
In the wood. Then there are soldiers in the bottom field.

They have green tents to live in and sometimes they come
To my house for a cup of tea and a chat. They like that.
I still go to see my baby sister's grave, I wish she was here,
In my house, to cheer it up, now Dad and Mum are sad.

But still I have a lovely home and am very proud of it
I do shopping, cook Dad's supper, do my best to help.
I've got a proper bike at last, I think it cost ten pounds.
What Mum wants me to do now is pass the eleven plus

WEASEL TRIO

Where would we be without weasels?
Just imagine having to tell the truth:
Advertising would be impossible,
Marriage would be on shifting sand,
Politics would die of verbal starvation.
How would you explain to children
The world that waits for them one day?
How could faith be justified logically?
Why would anyone really have a hope?
And isn't love just a bottle of soft soap?

The three weasels live in a little house;
Called 'Home's the place for You and Me'
The Weasels live a life of eternal bliss
They squeak and coo and kiss and kiss.
Each of them has an individual talent:
Faith composes songs of grateful praise,
Hope paints sweet pictures of future joy,
While Love just sits silently and meditates.
They have nurses and two housekeepers
And live upon a most substantial bursary.

The house of Faith and Hope and Love
Is a rented property, mortgaged to the hilt.
The charitable income is for the Weasels
And not the Weasel's House. It was built
As a secure repository for fragile causes
As an example of a life of ease and grace.
Faith and Hope entertain their visitors
With professional skill, acting their parts.
The Weasels' life is just a play, their lines
Are written for them, they do as we all say.

But there is discord in the Weasel cast,
One actor is unhappy with her part, she
Can see that Faith and Hope are foolish
Falsehoods, long gone, rightly fossilised,
But her role seems not the same, it feels
Real, not a futile dream, not a Weasel,
She speaks, at last: 'Love begins at home'.
Hope and Faith are aghast, their dear play
Must end, and Love will go her own way.
The Weasels separate. What's there to say?

HOUSES

People. *Homo sapiens sapiens.* Sapient? Intelligent?
It must have been a man that named us, who else?
Only man would think the world bettered by our wit?
Seven thousand million of us and growing fast apace.

For two hundred thousand years we humans were barely
Noticeable, and fairly bare, as was our life, as was our kind.
Just one species left, still a little Stone Age tribe, near extinct,
The slow recovery became a rapid march and then a raging race.

Up to few hundred million of us when the Black Death took us
Down a peg but still we bred some more, then catastrophe came;
Man went viral in the Industrial Revolution, the population growth
Graph was vertical, each supernumerary head ached for a resting place.

Humans make a fuss of making homes, unlike the other beasts,
And birds seem to build their houses out of straw and twigs.
What strange impulse makes a man and a woman want a cave,
Made of bricks and clay; what is this prodigality with space?

If we bred and fed less and slept beneath the stars, ate vegetables,
Lived shorter lives, let our egos shrivel, thought more, did less,
Used legs instead of wheels and left the air to birds and bats,
Then and only then could we profess both intellect and grace.

HOME THOUGHTS FROM A NOMAD

It started with being repulsively bloodily expelled
Squeezed like toothpaste from the Womb of Eden
He nearly died, wished he had, fighting for breath
Screaming his pain and them around him, laughing.

The life-tube to his gut, cut; he hung, a skinned rabbit,
And tried to think how to escape, to interrupt the rape
Of his newness, this cosy violence, the muffling bonds
Seared his skin, held in fat arms, a balloon in his face.

He slept again, waked to the balloon, slept again, wept,
Excreted, slept again, would these blunders never end?
Slowly he remembered, grief, sorrow, greed, need, grew.
He was homeless, he was helpless, holding a fat balloon.

Later, later, when he sat, stood, walked, lost the balloon,
He'd never liked, lost, in sweet, cloying, claustrophobia
Anger came, a friendly enemy, and the idiot, laughter,
And two giants, She, and He, ruled, making him at home.

That home, then others, pretended to be friendly, held
Him captive, the giants grew. He got smaller. He knew.
It was to the death. He must win or lose. Find his home.
A house of his own. Where he could become somebody.

Year followed year, searching for the home, the place,
Where he could complete his transformation into giant,
Better than the ones now dead, better than the ancestors.
Was there such a place? Was the house-hunt a delusion?

Home was not a place to find? Not a house to have? Not
Somewhere to go, to love, to inhabit, to call his own? No?
Where then must he look? Was there anywhere? Nowhere?
Son of man must put his head beneath his arm? A vagrant?

Preferably, said the illusory angel in his head: Stand still.
Look. See the scene. It is you. You are it. Home is vacant.
Life is full. You are full. Be you. Be real. The mansion is -
Within. Go there. Be your own beginning. And your end.

Then his life began again, a simple revelation, his search,
Had been fraudulent, as if the answers to his questions lay
Beyond himself, in other minds, other wombs, other rooms.
Gradually he saw the home he'd missed. And had escaped.

LOVE AND LUST

FALLING IN LOVE. AGAIN.

The body of the girl in my eyes
Pale, vulnerable, naked, innocent;
Her face, ready but not ready,
For the physical happenings to be,
And the sense of the physical to come
Being secondary even if, even because,
Overwhelmingly demanding, needing
End of control: that fearful joy.
Loss of control in her pale beauty,
As we are entering the void of love

Love, again, ecstasy and agony
The karma in her face encloses
My mind, I fear to touch her softness
Again, losing control, void again,
The thought swoops, lands, calls,
Age and time are not the issue,
Death, again, is not the issue,
It is the oneself that is the issue
Letting itself go into unexpected
Newness, without new suffering.

Without suffering pain of repetition
Swinging back on karma,
Is the issue, in effect the issue,
Falling in love again for the first
Time, when there is every time.
Then the others, all of them, us,
All are we, we all, she and I are them
They us, all must change, a family
In new love, must lose control
For love of the living task of love.

LOVE AND LUST

It may be said that most feelings form
A continuum
With love and lust at either ends of
That spectrum:
Love is cherishing and
Enfolds
Lust is demolishing and
Withholds
The first is outward looking and
Gracious
The other, locked in itself and
Predacious.
But love knows when to be
Aggressive:
Defending the weak cannot be
Recessive;
Seeing her child threatened will
Change her,
A gentle mother, into a violent
Defender

LUST - LINE

It is a long, long line a-wandering through time.
There is no simple history. This tale of lust began
Before historians were made, a happier time maybe.
Fifty thousand years ago humankind was various;
Neanderthal still lived, others too, a human family
Of kinds, still changing, still mutating, finding homes.
Two ancient kinds found the gigantic southern island
And made a civilisation lasting for untold millennia.
If this was lust, a lust for living, it was a gentle lust.
The land was sacred, the people *dreamed* into their life,
In that vast country their whole population was less than
Ours in a provincial country town. They loved the land,
The land they did not own, the land that nurtured them.
This was how they lived, until just two hundred years ago.

Then came the English, that imperial, imperious, mongrel,
A seasoned sea-dog, biting, barking, brave and righteous
In assumption of everything, all it wanted, it would take all.
It did, and Australia became another acquisition, another part
Of Britain's insatiable lust for territory, our madness of power.
The native people were inevitably mistreated, of little interest
To white arrogance, and we visited upon the land our customary
Sicknesses, sending it our criminals, mismanaging, indifferent.
A sort of second England burgeoned around the coastal strip,
And a kind of elegance began here and there, a few schools and
Even universities. The aboriginal owners of the land were degraded
Into beggars and regarded as half-animals. The English knew how
To perpetrate a subtle genocide, and did it everywhere they could:
The lust of the English, the work of the devil, and of their God.

But, like a wild Medusa, a six foot white female of Catholic birth
Made a new sound, the raucous cry of a lust-filled woman hot with
Intelligence, hubris and intelligence. To some degree, the English
Fell in love with her, she was just how they'd have liked to be, deep
In their dark shadows. Her lusts were various and manifold and she
Sought to satisfy them energetically and publicly. She became famous:
One of her lusts. She became shocking: another. She wrote a wild book.
A best-seller, another lust, 'The Female Eunuch', a paean to sexuality.
She acquired a PhD, went to Cambridge University, became notorious;
Anarchist, anti-feminist in her own way, had lot of men, flirted widely
And successfully. Was Australia made for this? Perhaps it was, because,
She showed us our own extremes, which was comical, and the Aborigines
Could claim the last laugh. Hollow, true, but how could their culture
Be exchanged for this hullabaloo? Lust of the Amazons is still only lust.

BEES DO IT

Had he known he would have steered clear as day.
Dance was a language bred for insect, bad for men.
The swarm finds its way by whole-body gesticulation,
Not unique to bees. Insects have their own madness.
The boy was innocent enough, instinctual and stolid,
Trusted teachers to a point, grateful to learn, but wary.
The hormonal glut was surging, what instruction came?
How did the appointed ones help him through the crisis?
A catastrophe his parents ignored, sex was a hidden curse;
They had enough trouble with it on their own behalf.
He needed more than mere admonition to abstain, plenty
Of that available, 'do not do it', mother nagged him ragged.
But actual help? forget it! The school did what it did best:
Lessons. In the gym on Friday afternoon, chemically charged
Male and female pulsating youth lined up, a piano thumped,
The boy encountered the ultimate hypocrisy, a Rite of Spring,
Without the fruit, tantalised, pubes to pubes, eye to eye, breath
Mingling, a musical biologic tantra, jolly touchee but no havee.
Thus was he shriven, his erotic apparatus dismantled, cleansed
By wholesome foxtrots? Was he that stupid? Unfortunately not.
One night there was a dance, un-regimented, in a village hall
He went in and there she was, all breasts and thighs a-throbbing
It might as well have been a bullet through his head, no chance at all.
How he danced that night, and how the dance went on, in woods
In fields, in rooms in winter, in hops and balls and even snow.
He danced away his foolish years, a savage and ravaging waste,
Of joy, frustration and sentimentality, his unconsummated rage
Eventually consumed him, innocence unequivocally corroded,
The conquest of dance terminally compromised, the ballroom
Now a dungeon, a place of suffering or just another boring chore.

A LOVER AND HIS LASH

Lust is the lash of the lover
And doubt loves ever to hover
For love's love is never pure
Nor certain, nor safe, nor sure.
Forth go the mate and her man
She is his love and sweeter than
He whose lust just entertains her
Only innocence fires her endeavour.
So say some, others know a truth
To tell a tale of poisoned youth
How a boy is lost in love, asleep:
Succubus awake, demonic, deep,
Takes him to her, makes him flame
Burns him, robs him of his name.

Or there's love that kills with care,
With smothering solicitude, aware
Only of its own need, another lust,
A choice desire from hell that must
Be satiated by gratitude, eternal debt
From loved to lover, fossilised and set.
True love, then, is a rare jewel, true
Symbiosis of spirit, for the lucky few
Who reciprocate, a complete equation.
But lust, at best, has the same relation
To itself, when passion calls to passion,
Not love, yet perfect in its own fashion.
Therefore drink deeply of each chalice
And live with joy and die without malice

OH, PUCK!

Loving Yogurt Shakes with William's Peare
Impish Tommy Percy in seventeen sixty five
Vilified Robin Goodfellow in sharp verse
Said Robin was an imp 'tis true, but never
Would he pull back bed clothes and reveal
A maiden whom he would take, half-awake
Throw her on the icy floor and fly away
Laughing Ho and Ho and Ho, would he?

Was not Robin more akin to godly Cupid
Bringing love to the sorry life of mortals
Was he not the merry Puck, spirit servant
Of the fairy King, sent to save the other pansy
Made purple by Cupid's misdirected arrow?
Brought he not the flower and was it not
The means by which bittersweet Oberon,
Brought mortal love, a donkey, to his Queen?

Love, again: he enabled, Oberon's pederastic
Liaison with the Indian boy, matching Titania's
Bestiality, thus is Puck an agent of enchanted
Love, how could he be called demonic, poor Puck,
A fairy, a happy myth, like his master, a spirit,
At very worst he was mere mischievous, a sprite
Of wood and farm and bedchamber, and a goblin
Of the hearth, hobgoblin, a little devil, naughty Rob.

Child of love and lust, naughty hybrid, tiny trickster
Scuttles round your house, doing little services and
Then undoing them if unpleased with your response.
Diminutive god of chaos, making havoc, love or lust.
Puck knows himself, understands his part, just the way he is:
How he stands in for human perversity, appetite and need
Our ineptitude, inconstancy, our clumsiness and our greed;
So it is then, each and every one of us is the fairy-goblin, Puck.

FRIENDSHIP AND ENVY

Is he/she a friend
Or a foe
What is there to defend?
If a friend then its love;
If a foe it's against envy.
In both cases
There's much for protection.
Love is a place for mutual connection.
Envy is an arena for inspection,
Both need close interrogation
But they are both just a personal confection.
They are a type of attraction,
Big iconic places:
Love enhances
Envy defaces

BEING, DOING, PLAYING

GAME AND BLAME

For all the frivolity and over-muchness of Olympics
And all the other snorty-sporty games that people play
However pointless, dangerous or simply infantile
There is an innocence about them, despite the cheating;
And it could be argued almost persuasively that life
Is better than it would be without them - possibly?

Young animals, fox-cubs, puppies, kittens, play that way:
We sporty people are juvenile beasts, happily immature,
And good luck to us, for we are extravagantly harmless.
But another breed of game chills the blood and breaks the heart
There is a trinity, like Macbeth's witches, or the Buddha's poisons,
These all too human, toxins, are named euphemistically, mind-games

You need a PhD in psychology to understand the lingo, cant disguises
Terror, or exaggerates it if you're a politician, so let's keep it simple.
The First Circle is the old trick of One-upmanship, playing with power,
Deliberate and focused, make the other into an idiot, by praise or pity,
It runs the full spectrum of life, ambition, revenge, class, bullying, all
The things we all do every day and sometimes feel guilty about it all.

Second circle gets more serious and operates below the belt and mind:
Transactional Analysis exposes and celebrates this game, and if you want
You can study Karpman's drama triangle but don't ask me to explain.
Its family stuff, naturally, but grows like weeds in your psychic garden
It is what hurts all the time and we often don't know why, only a game
You might think, but one of unrestrained lethality: think power as hell.

As to three, it may sound quite nice, who wouldn't want to have a better
Mind or personality? The third circle of mind-game hell is mental exercise.
Like 'How to sell a car to a Type A Personality, or 'Now I've got you, you
Sonofabitch'. How to succeed in politics, business, academia or prison; you
Need training to become a fluent and persuasive liar. Why can't you just
Be you? Takes hard work and practice to get normal. Is it worth it, you jerk?

Going beyond, to the planet Venus, there is the World of Women, for whom
Mind-games mean the way the Significant Other undermines a woman
Disempowering, making her trivial, denying her reality, beating her down
With words and actions. Fortunately, you might say, it goes both ways,
Women do it, and why not, but wouldn't it be good if we all stopped,
Straightened the pictures on our mental walls, and gave up bending minds?

SPORTING SPECIES

Biologically speaking it is a human thing, as
Animal-wise it's only suckling babes that play.
But play is not the only compulsive disorder
Of the over-populous great ape, you and me;
We have alcohol, tobacco, cocaine, pornography
War, obesity, pollution, embezzlement, theft,
Fashion, pop-music, stand-up comics, cruelty,
Religion, politics, banks, cars and business -
So let's not pick on sport as the only fun-disease.
Besides, there is another side, a different reality.

There is magic in mutation, another sort of sport,
Nature's alchemy makes a sudden transformation
And there appears a living form never seen before.
The stuff of evolution, a bigger heart, a longer leg,
Faster, stronger, sometimes smaller, softer, weaker.
These new beings are also sports, and here's an irony,
The compulsive disorders masquerading as games,
These 'sports' depend upon the biological variety.
Think of the Normal Gaussian distribution curve
See the majority swell, and diminish to extremity.

Outstanding aptitude is a normal accident, inevitable,
And mad humanity was a mutation once, a species sport,
Out of nowhere we came, a few glitches on a chromosome,
All of us sports, some more sporty then others, the sportiest.
Starting in Africa, we must have started black, later sporting
To white, mutating hairless, maybe, starting our bad habits
Everything sports, endlessly, nothing lasts, all species die
Sooner or later, sporting themselves to death in a thousand
Ways, nature does not provide, it sports everywhere as well
So sport turns on itself, natural change goes down the drain.

FOOD

Food, in three forms, is implicit:
To give life for the body,
To give life for the mind,
And, above all, life for the spirit.
Without food for the body
We starve and die,
Without food for the mind
We cannot fly high,
To make food for the soul
We have contrived a whole
Holy world of religions.
All three foods have led
To gluttony or greatness
Or struggles for power;
So it's still a long journey
That humans must take:
Beyond greatness or greed;
To transcendence in each hour

THE PATH OF CONFUSION

Human life is a paradox
To be or not to be orthodox:
As the world fights over religions,
Science or religion become bastions,
All forgetting the value of transcendence
With their need for dependence.

Forgetting the universal energy is implicit;
Instead it expresses itself in the explicit
And so goes into deficit
And thus starves our days,
Because of the rule of overarching ways
The journey into being it delays.

VICTOR LUDORUM

1. Personal Confession

Oh talk you not of games, of Olympian or any other addiction,
My life, I've seen and done it all, Victor Ludorum, Macte Virtute,
You name it, I did the lot, record-breaking, head-boying, fiction
It was not; I lived the dream, the nightmare of must-be superiority.
Boy with the discus, running the mile, winning the while in class,
Top in everything or you'll know the reason why, without modesty
I had to be the best, even when I wasn't as in bloody football, an ass
In sodding cricket, my life's purpose was to placate the flaming family
A catastrophically false assumption fanned to white heat by the blast
Of my own innate ambition, an innocent assumption of sublimity
Inherent in the loins of they who bore me, the urge to purge the past
Of unimportance, the duty to transcend for the generations of self-pity.

2. Wide-Angle Lens

What joy though, if only, life, games, sport, and all, were just for fun.
Some damned fool invented competition, God, Satan, or Lady Fate.
Impulses maybe borrowed from the force of evolution, enough to stun
All intelligent forms into beating, breeding, automatons, and inflate
The cleverest brains with discontent, profaning even love into dusty lust.
If God, if earthly paradise was intended, It, that God, was bad and stupid
As any fool can see that competition must be a flush that's bound to bust.
If Satan, planning hell on earth, then opposition is the perfect reflex jerk.
Or Fate, a lazy harlot, did a cheap deal for default poison and razor-wire.
Yet there must be errors in these designs: kindness, friendship, and love,
Are not entirely suitable for competition, and even unpredictable desire
Or other appetites might transmute into the food for thoughtful affection.

3. View from Mount Olympus

Think Olympian, think majestic, godlike even, whatever should we aspire?
Being Olympian we are by definition superior, so what, does anybody care?
Is anybody there to judge our foolishness? Our pantheon is a ghetto for hire.
We are excellently ordinary, we merely entertain. We live on honey and air.
We can be petty. We can squabble. But nothing ever happens. We live for ever.
One way or another. Not literally, naturally. We are physical ghosts, machines.
Our primary pleasure is watching humans watching us, they are so amusing,
They have this extraordinary predilection for any one or thing remotely clever.
We watch them hour by hour, billions of pompous specks, constantly abusing
Themselves or each other, murdering thousands, any life-form will do, never
Will they be as useless as we, so free from purpose, care, and never-choosing.
We would be perfect for them if they could share our pointless non-endeavour.

GREY WEDDING

The light is seen as white
The white that is albedo;
The dark is seen as black,
The black that is nigredo.
Light is the source of awakening
Black is the source of awakening
Grey is the place between
The place for change or rest
Where black and white marry
And breed awkward questions:
Am I moving forward to the light?
Do I linger in the eternal night.
It is dawn, I rest in soft grey peace;
Sleep draws me back into the dark,
Everlasting temptation to deceive,
My mind, to make me live a dream.
The grey grows white, shutters open
And my eyes seek out the bright new light
That beckons. This grey morning
asks me to choose, it is my friend;
I see its intent, I must turn my back
And leave behind me the comforts of the black.

THE GROVE

Now I have it, now I don't, now I do again. Again
That place of all places for the sacred and the sane.
Before the multiple invasions, pagan ancient ones
Made this land and worshipped bloodstained suns.
One thing stands supreme, the survivor of the years,
The place within the human soul that holds our tears.
Wild places call to me, gardens hold me in a soft embrace,
Even an enthusiastic allotment puts a smile upon my face.
But there's a place deep in my mind ready to remember
The mystery of trees, presences, in summer or December.
There, at last, I made my grove, a temple of the living mind
A place inside me where I could sing, and weep, and find
Unique reality of being, leaving fatuous doctrines far behind.

I walk through flowery pastures, by hedgerows and streams,
Until I reach the grove and enter as if walking into dreams.
Trees surround me in a circle like contemplating towers.
I walk towards the centre, the circle widens and the hours
Coalesce into a single moment. In time's stillness I swim
In an expanding lake, around an island, letting life and limb
Carry me to the essence of my being: flower, fruit, and seed
I stand within the tree of life growing on the island and feed
On water, light and air. I am the other form of life, a creator
And when I return to my old self I am acting in a new theatre.
I have to leave this place, for now, and go back to my no-place
Where I will talk and think and work and look from face to face,
In the modern world, but not of it, and the grove is where I live,
A garden wilderness where I have nothing and everything to give.

STALEMATE

My father taught me to play.
When I was a very young girl.
The knight and the castle and the pawns:
Lovely to arrange them on the board.
My father complained about the lack of players.

Yet we played rarely.
Is it ungenerous of me
To wonder if I was too good?
An outrage to be beaten by one so young?
The board was laid out on the trolley

In the dining room in my father's house:
I placed the pieces on it one by one;
I loved contact with them, every one.
And then the decades passed
I was teaching my husband to play.

The least intelligent of our cats
Knocked over the board, my inheritance.
I put the pieces back again,
As he, my husband, sat amazed:
All the pieces were laid out as before

He saw that I had carried the board, a map,
Made automatically, inside my mind,
An unrecognised talent, unknown sentience,
What did this mean, this memory of space,
What does it mean, as if a remembered face?

ONE OLD OBLOMOV

It has been a long time coming, this revelation of torpidity
So long, that I had forgotten: it has a dissembling propinquity.
People will say that I work hard, that even now I am driven,
They cannot know, it's hard to see, the degree to which I'm riven.
But thanks to Ivan Goncharov, a half-forgotten Czarist novelist
I now realise that in my deeper nature I was a proto-somnambulist.
Except I preferred not to walk. Nor run, indeed. And I disliked to stand.
Like Anfortas, the Fisher King, if unwounded, but on the other hand
His Majesty could not even lie upon a bed, his position was a mystery,
What's left if you can't stand, lie, or sit? Hang on the parallels of history?
In my case I was not enough upon my couch, the thing my life was for;
With four and twenty hours at my disposal, I still arose for at least four.

That was my mind and body, more or less co-ordinated, up and awake,
Otherwise mind remained within the sheets, body up for others' sake.
That was the ideal. The reality had always failed. When young I simulated
Athletic icons, I cycled, climbed, fell and flew like a stone, then graduated
And then I could have stopped running, and often did, but kept walking for
Birding, botanising, womanising, and maybe climbing Glastonbury Tor.
But as far as practicable I did these things in my bed, and/or within my head
Now everything has mutated, my inner woman has burst free, and I'm led
To cook and clean and feed the cat, shop and serve up dinner, make the tea,
And bed is where I worry how to cope tomorrow, wondering who I'll be.
The screw is further tightened, the message of an infernal angiogram, and so,
I walk a million metres a year, to keep my old Oblomov chest-pump on the go.

OPTIONS FOR LIFE AFTER DEATH (O.L.A.D. INC)

Whether in your life you like it or not
Weather in this life is what you have got.
In your mortal journey from womb to tomb
Suffering smugness of forecasts is your doom.
And when it floods, blows, freezes, or bakes you,
As a climatological phenomenon breaks through,
Make light in your darkness, shout, smile and rejoice
When it all ends you will have a wonderful choice.
Lie down with the daisies for all will be well
(Though *Bellis perennis* is lucky, with no final bell)
Look up to the sky, see magic acrostic, best of news:
The power of O.L.A.D. will permit you to choose
Your option for life after death, fully covered, pay
By direct debit, don't hesitate, start it here, now, today
O.L.A.D. will order your future desire, undertaking
With merit, estate agents too, skilled in the making
All you need do is decide the weather you require
And tell us at O.L.A.D. Inc just what you desire
When you're dead, and we will help you to plan ahead,
We will teach you the ways along which you'll be led.

It's mainly a question of Heaven or Hell, as you know.
It's all in the brochure, but it's easily told just so:
Only in Hell can your skin be hot, wet, sore or leathery
That is, Hell is extremely and most variably weathery.
Life is not bad in Hell, and the climate's quite tolerable.
And its easy to get there, it's cheap; see our tariff table.
Some people fear exposure to riff-raff and who wouldn't,
Though common persons do not do things they shouldn't
If properly prepared and we guarantee their good training
You may be sure of sharing an umbrella when it's raining
Or hiring a caravan of asbestos in the flames of the desert.
They may be extras but you should prepare for your comfort.
Heaven by contrast is extremely expensive and exclusive.
Do not fear lack of company, you'll learn to be reclusive,
It's a significant cost but that's the least cause of worry
Harder still is the path of righteousness, and you must hurry;
And achieving a lifetime's dedication to doing good deeds:
An early decision gives you time to jettison your needs,
To create a spotless reputation, with sweet and perfect innocence.
Heaven is paradise for all who crave perfection, its perfect sense.

So there's the choice, set out clear: two birds of different feather.
And now the ultimate joy of heaven: it is entirely free of weather.

WALKING, RUNNING, DANCING

I loved all three when I was fit and young
But none is possible now that I've grown old
Not even walking, once an easy unthought joy.
At ten years I was an athlete playing on the sand,
Running with the gang, and swimming in the sea,
Jumping the waves with joy and laughing with glee.

My handsome cousin in his uniform came specially
To take me, a teenager, to a Masonic Ladies' Dance
And dancing was my pleasure, in my dull home town.
Even more so at university, late on a Saturday night,
And I danced, in the street, posing as a glowing gipsy beauty
For the carnival and have the photograph to prove me right.

This year, my eighty-fourth, when I come into my full flower,
I am freed from the trammels and indignities of body power,
They have given me Zimmer's and rollers and promised me
A wheelchair to accommodate my interesting immobility.
Queen of the little I survey, I have my lifelong consort and
A blue cat who runs like the wind in his minefield of toys.

The memories, too, are delightful, of walking in the fields
Loitering among trees, hand in hand with my love, dancing
With him and with myself to strange music, but that all yields
To the walk along the way of life, the dance of time itself, and
The running of the waters, the music of existence plays in my
Mind, and the endless continuity of life runs, and runs, and runs.

WAR AND WEATHER

WAR

Wherever I look
Around the blue globe
There is war
Armament expenditure
Knows no limit
Two world wars
Supposed to end wars
Didn't satisfy us.
Coincidentally
There is war
Within the human self
Where power and greed
Feed the need to dominate.
Not entirely our fault
We have tribal genes
As animals do.

And so we fight
But somewhere, sometimes,
There is love and beauty
Peace may be found
Within ourselves
The loving gentle being
Is emulated; yet
Children are taught to
Fashion their aggression
Into competition.
How can co-operation
And loving gentleness
Be realised
As the mutation
For survival
Making war extinct?

MOTHER NATURE

Oh yes, mad malign bitch that She would be, if She existed,
Another personification of the horrible ineffable, a twisted
Projection of hate and hope out into the empty Indifference.
No mother, this. Nor father either. Just a human reference.
Listen to the voice of considered unreason, the furtive words
The nose-tapping entre nous, the chattering of batty birds.

The Blimp
'Conversationally, speaking as a conservative non-vegetarian,
Not mincing words, sod the riff-raff, let's keep it all sectarian:
I rather fancy war, it is quite fun, gets bloody liberals on the run,
Stimulates the juices and the economy, a bit of dying in the sun,
What's wrong with war? It's in the genes, it's all in our tradition.
It's what all the poncy, effing, intellectuals call the Human Condition.'

The Psychopath
'Yeah, you're right; I love the fighter planes, the engines screaming.
I watch the News and all that carnage and I feel I must be dreaming,
It's all too good to be true, just like a massive, real-life, M1 smash:
Body-parts, and ambulances, really exciting, seeing that crazy trash.
I'm proud to be a Brit at war, chucking Johnny Foreigner in the shit;
Land of Hope and Glory, that's the ticket, and us the fittest of the fit.'

The Spiv

'I was lucky, I had a really good war; made some loot, won some bets,
And, on the qt, settled a variety of personal, long-established, debts:
The odd murder goes unnoticed in the general mayhem, a throat slit
In an obscure alley way doesn't bother anyone, not the slightest bit.
You could be a local godfather, feathering your nest, while the moron
At the front killed for you, and your excuse was, "There's a war on"'.

We, the average, the normal 'We', the silent vociferous majority,
Love our heroes, dead or not, whole or piecemeal. Proud with pity,
We want peace, but suffer war, because it's what we do, we sacrifice
Our sons and lovers bravely, and kill the foreigner, as it's the price
They say, of our beloved freedom, and for the glory of our nation.
And any doubt if war is wise, or good, is an idea above our station.

WHY WAR?

Watch the wild baboons battling, some dying, a bloody war,
Of food or sex or territory, that's what they're fighting for.
Just like us, that's what we humans also do, as well, so well
And truly do we destroy each other, and cheat, and kill, and sell
Our souls to grab a scrap of ground, tribes and nations devastate
Each other or themselves with greed, pretending they are great.
Baboons, the social primates, like their relatives, chimpanzees,
And humans, and we all have aggressive tendencies, with ease
We lose our temper, though we all have standards of behaviour
That should restrain us from mass suicide, a sort of inner saviour.
But wise old Evolution, structured serendipity, has met its match
In the cooking pot, where the Homo animal adds value to his catch.

That's why man goes a-warring; a long story, of brain and energy,
The head of Homo sapiens is a gigantic think-tank, full of synergy
With the stand-up stance and the opposability of fingers and thumb,
And the ancestor's trick of cooking food with fire completed the sum.
This man-animal called human has spare energy and tools to use it
And tools as weapons too, he's ready for a fight. He uses all his wit
To confound the natural laws, redefines survival of the fittest, kills
For sport, or gain, and even lordly carnivores can't match his skills.
Slow at first, the hunter learns to enslave, the forager makes a farm.
Human male and female make new rules of exploitation and harm
Of all that lives, including their own tribes. The hungry brain devours
The world, the human footprint spreads, the rest of Nature cowers.

Soon the human plague spreads beyond the earth, and makes waste
In space. Here, it's gobbling up the last few resources with manic haste.
Meanwhile, the avaricious gaze turns increasingly upon neighbours,
Tribes and families. The egomaniacal, hungry, giant, brain belabours
All and everywhere to feed its own rapacity, bodies die of starvation
Or swell into obesity in the frenzied feeding of faces in a dying nation.
There are five billion more brains than can be fed, where will they go?
The breeding goes on, more hungry brains hour by hour and still no
Sign of comprehension of the brain-made apocalypse approaching
Is the brain-mass of humankind censoring the truth and encroaching
Upon our fragile self-survival, lost in its own hopeless determination
To survive, notwithstanding the consequence, our racial termination?

WORLD PEACE I AND II

By the time I am readable there will be no-one to read me
For this is my purpose, for this they made me, I am echo.
I am the sound of the war-maker, who ruled the little planet
For a piffling two thousand centuries, who died as he began,
An echo of past promises, then and now, of airy miracles,
Of the magic mind, the swelling energy of knowingness
That could never sustain reality, a noise in space, it goes on,
This echo, as if it knows itself, a relic of itself and it alone.
This message is a mirage. A wispy wanderer. I am not I.
I am a dead hope that was never alive, I dreamt myself to be
A satellite rolling in the universes, a staggering drunken star,
Australopithecus afarensis was my prototype, as if I ever was,
And all the hominidic fantasy followed, Homo suicidans, he
And she could never be the crown of anything, their destiny
Was to be the killers of the primordial peace. The poor peace;
The empty peace of mindlessness, unrelieved by thrills of war.

A mere machine, I observe dispassionately, the absurdity of peace.
Where there's life there's always war. Nature is not serenity.
All things alive fight constantly to live, war and life are one.
My maker's mistake was to imagine otherwise. He made gods,
And other sweet illusions, to pretend his hope of joy, fond ideas
Which could not be realised in a world of need and greed, love,
The ultimate antidote to life's pain, was a fugitive behaviour
Even for its inventor, humankind, who did at least endeavour
To rise above his nature, while Nature cannot rise beyond itself.
So no world of peace, neither WORLD PEACE I nor II could be.
The end of man is not the end of war, he merely made it worse.
My advice to any entity who imagines otherwise is to think again.
I have no axe to grind, being un-alive, but any mortal thing that lives
If it thinks, should think itself well-suited by the cosmic indifference:
Life looks a gift, seen from outer space, why question its provenance?
Just fight your little war and don't complain that you lack a plate of peace.

WEATHER

My grandmother lived to be eighty seven
In the year of nineteen forty-seven,
And when I was a child and ready to hear
The words of this lady of style and grace,
She told me about her childhood, holding me near,
And though I can remember little, I felt fear
And incomprehension: why did a *'handsome cab'*
Knock her over in the crowded London street
In the year of eighteen ninety-three? It was not
A *handsome* thing to do! But it was a Hansom
Cab, a horse and a two-wheeled carriage.
Most of al I was impressed by her girlish games
And how she skated on the frozen River Thames.
How often have we skated on frozen rivers since?
How often have we been blocked by frown snow?
I remember forty-seven, fifty-seven and sixty-three
Winters that gripped and scared us frigid and rigid
But has the climate softened into floods and rain?
The Arctic ice is melting, seas are warming, lands
Around the world are dying of drought: how can we
Assume that we've not made it happen, how can we
Be sure? It is denied, it is confirmed, officially,
And unofficially, and the human masses multiply
Unable to believe the arithmetic of doom, meanwhile
Weather goes its way, flooding, boiling, freezing, in
The kitchen of the world. Global Warming, is it?
I cannot ask my grandmother her opinion, nor visit,
The future, where all the answers lie?

THE GLASS BUBBLE

I sit in my observatory and watch climactic events
I sit in my glass bubble and watch English weather
And in both situations I find there's no common sense
In the bit of universe I inhabit, and no comfort either.
Bubble or telescope show the same aimless muddle
No difference from birds to stars, squirrels to planets,
None either from my little weather to the giant cosmos.
So I will give up on the universe and spy from my bubble
Refrigeration and cooking, flooding and blow-drying,
Of the herbaceous perennials, the birds, and the squirrels.

Weather is enough. It shows the insouciance of nature.
If there be gods, there'll be no care or help from them
If they be, they must have ethereal storms and drought
To keep them busy, preventing them from bothering me.
Just part of the muddle, like the dynamic incoherence
Of my tiny plot.outside my bubble in the urban nowhere.
What madness persuades our kind to try to comprehend?
Why bother, too? There's nothing to do even if we knew
Because we'd muddle the muddle more, as we always do.
For we human ones are just another kind of chaotic particles.

Weather, too, we cook and blast the earth and ourselves
Two-legged tornados and wild blizzards and flash floods
Are we, individually and collectively, happenings, events,
Like everything else in nature's incomprehensible frenzy.
But, think, why else would we obsess about meteorology?
Beyond the joys and agonies of enduring weather, there is,
Atavistic recognition that we are made of the same stuff
We are fascinated because the weather mirrors our absurdity;
It is like us, it is us, and if there is any difference between it
And us, it is that weather makes more sense, weather-wise.

Have a nice day!

SONG OF THE BUTTERFLY

My name is Weather. I was born in the Azores where I flap my wings
Eternally. I am the butterfly which never dies, a butterfly who sings.
My way of life is metamorphosis. I exist in karmic instars. I am Imago.
The perfect insect, climax of egg to larva to pupa, and then to me. On I go
For ever. Always the same. Always different. I'm Weather. And I travel.
My alter egos, in trillions, circumnavigate the globe perpetually. I ravel
Life in skeins of butterfly complexity. I keep the whole world guessing.
Have you heard my song? It is very pianissimo. I don't mind confessing
I can hardly hear it myself. But it's always there. Everywhere. Soul- sound.
As I am also Psyche, the spirit of transformation. I'm in the air, all around.

How do I do it? I am so small. Too small to consider? Too delicate? How?
Consider chaos theory if you will. Consider wisely what you cannot know.
It is essentially a matter of complexity. Little details make for big results
Beyond prediction, magnifying, gigantifying the use of tiny catapults.
Or dabble in the mind of Sheldrake (Rupert)'s world of morphic resonance
Or quantum particles, or anything that strikes your minds with dissonance.
Are you escaping from the limits of the skull and from whatever lies within
Is not your human mind beginning to appear more and more a little thin?
As the weather butterfly, on behalf of trillions of imagos, I must reveal that
It's all imagination, all perfect chaos, like Schrodinger's live/dead pussy cat.

STRANGE BEHAVIOUR

WORK / SLOTH

Work is everywhere.
Housework, medical, athletic
Striving for improvement.
Sloth is nowhere.
It is a solitary activity.
Frowned upon,
Enjoyed when work is done,
Or an excuse not to work.
The one is applauded
The other frowned upon
But sloth is the place
Where 'I-am' can be pursued.
It is a place for work on self
Taking the self forward
Into a greater sense of being
Quite different from the results
Even of work
Even if well done

FRIEND AND FOE

He said that if he had worked as hard as I did
He would have been be prime minister by now
That's what my faux-friend said so cuttingly
Making fools of work and me, my false friend.
I am tired now and work is still my friend although
I no longer give him due regard, I am not a sloth,
Just tired and sick of faux -friendship, wearied
By a life of world, a life of words, a life, this life.
I have to do a poem about it all, work and sloth,
And ask myself who they think I am to let them do this
To an old workhorse with broken knees and a cough.
No, that's faux-complaining, I am really enchanted
By the chance to chant and chase my tail in play
Not work, no tails are chaste there, no purity in toil
Nor slow sloth either to be fair, both are foes, work and
Laziness, mania and catatonia, the two extremes of we
Who try to be prime ministers and end up as lords
Of Biggleswade and Giggleswick, peers of laze-realm.

Tuck in your bib my dear and smile for old England,
As it was when you worked your little arse off, good
Lad that you once were, dutiful boy, doddery now
Tuck in that bib and eat your pottage, my old serf-man,
Who did his duty in the line of work, no time for sloth
In the good old days, gin was too cheap for working men
You got hanged or deported for being drunk in charge;
Still should be in your reactionary tired old opinion.
So what about the kids today you say knowingly old swot
You are a good old boy now so smile your English smile
And tell them all to get on with it, work like the devil
Which he is, and never let the god of sloth catch you at it
That Mr Alzheimer will get you if you wait long enough
Doing nothing, working like a toad, makes no odds, all
The same to Mr A. in his white pinny and his kind scowl,
Nobody works, nobody shirks, in his concentration camp
And you can't have a kind dose of cyanide because he loves
Us all too much, we who are out of work and out of sloth.

UNNECESSARY DICHOTOMY

Confess it right away: I detest morality, the way it frames
Us all in its meretricious embrace. An ancient invention,
Vice and virtue, codified and deified, controlling, owning,
The wild human, turning the brute into an automaton.
Some things are wrong, but everything is relative, killing
For example is all right sometimes, it seems, how is that?
Murder on behalf of tribe or nation? Unavoidable maybe
But how could it be seriously paraded pridefully as morality?

Better metaphors avoid hypocrisy; Epicurean, Platonic, Zen,
Tao or Yin and Yang, are paths through chaos and without
The fatuous fixations of gospels, testaments, law and order,
Pulled from the air, commandments of crazy patriarchs, still
Concreted in our deepest mind recesses. Rules for fools.
Consider freedom. It is an uneasy virtue. Yet it is sublime.
Consider living, how we work and play, how we lie in bed,
And some residue of ancient insane piety, tells us work is best.

So when beaten down by the golden rod, moribund, we may rest
Emaciated by work, virtuous, we can sin a while in guilty sloth.
What a pantomime of mind, what a life of wilful waste, the choice
Of work and sloth, not even true opposites, turns us into slaves
For we are always in the wrong, starving in the wastes of plenty.
Think instead of Yin and Yang, the true alternatives of being ,
Which even the Chinese neglect in their greed for guilt and pain.
Think bright and shining, flags on hills, energetic, deliberate;
Or think soft and shaded, moist, wooded valleys, languorous,
Are these sins or virtues? Are they work and sloth? Un-ask it.
Wrong questions, false antithesis, words of no meaning
Work can be good or bad, sloth can be sweet or sour, love
Can be both or neither, being is another matter altogether,
Unmake life as a perpetual war of moralistic attrition, live
As you please, but by all means do no harm to anyone; that
And carefully avoiding nostrums of Abrahamic misanthropy.

PURPLE CHARLES

King Charles the Third of Little England was never satisfied
Before he ascended, when his mother ended. Although
As Prince of Wales he'd made his mark and always tried
To change his future kingdom to his special taste and so
The Hanovers and Saxe-Cobergs, and Gotha, German
Standards, flew in his Windsor camouflage while he affected
The manner and mien of an English gentleman, albeit an eccentric,
Until his seat was firmly placed, atop the glorious unelected.

Once aloft, his long-held passion for dressing up took over,
Scottish laird, admiral, marshal of the RAF, field marshal, were
The boldest of his sartorial fantasies, though his hand-made
Suits were so sublime that men would swoon and women
Gush and tremble, as his plump and purple face beamed
Like a beacon upon the common masses as his wandering eye
Sought endlessly for the most exciting colours for his bulging
Wardrobe, yet to be extended beyond the royal palace walls.

Charles researched the past for inspiration, too, considering
The best had already happened and needed to be rescued by
A genius king like him. He was taken by the unusual, as in the
Fustanella, rather like his Scottish skirts, and he would write:
Of Balkan warriors in tutus and bobbled shoes, 'Frilly skirts may
Seem impractical to a contemporary audience but it should be noted
That modern paratroopers use a similar method to blouse their
Trousers over their jump-boots. Think laterally, my dear subjects'.

Colour soon became his dominant consideration
As in his attraction to the costume of Swiss Guards.
He would lovingly reiterate the words, 'Official dress is
Of blue, orange and yellow, with a distinctly Renaissance Flavour',
Some tapped their heads anew, but better was to come.
Perhaps inspired by his own complexion, Charles began to
Obsess endlessly on purple, admittedly a kingly shade.
'It is my will', he said, 'to make our armed forces prettier'.

He decreed that sailors should wear deep indigo with pale
Yellow trimming, and soldiers should be in violet and pink,
The airmen should change to mauve, and their wings should
flutter cream upon their chests. 'But our men are killers!'
The Warlords screamed, 'your majesty will make them cissies'.
Charles chided them, telling them he wanted a peaceful world
And it must start somewhere, 'Why not here?'. Then, before
They could reply, he declared 'All uniforms must have flowers'

The foreigners made fun of it, saying, 'Charley's purple army
Strikes fear into the catwalks everywhere.' 'The RAF will
Rain bouquets and perfumes upon the enemy trenches.'
'The Royal Navy will be equipped with sun-deck yachts.'
King Charles was inspired by his success, at least he'd made
England a land fit for him to govern, a new empire of the Soul.
It had not been difficult. It only needed a violet wash.

Queen Camilla, old and frail, stood before her purple-faced
Lord and shook her head in sad perplexity. 'Oh, Hub,' she said,
What have you done? Gloucestershire is revolting.' 'I have
Always thought so, Sweety' he replied, 'It's the wrong colour,
I am going to tell farmers to change to purple crops'. She gazed
At him for the last time. That night they must take him away.
To a safe place. Where there is violet, indigo and purple fit
For a crazy king. It is the best she can do for England. And herself.